"Learn to recognize your inner stre[ngth and] loose negative distractions. Whe[n you do,] Bonnie Groessl opens an honest discussion with clear strategies for [those] who wish to direct their energy toward feeling good and much stronger. Guide your life path with these tools."

> -Jeffrey N. Gingold, author of the award-winning books, *Facing the Cognitive Challenges of Multiple Sclerosis* and *Mental Sharpening Stones: Manage the Cognitive Challenges of Multiple Sclerosis*.

"Bonnie Groessl has a wonderful way of showing all of us the gifts that we possess within us. Her book teaches us how to focus on the abundance that is present in our lives rather than what is missing. By following her guidance and techniques we can all experience a true self loving and appreciation for those around us. Everyone that has been searching for a better quality of life, emotionally, financially, spiritually, or physically should read this book."

> -Traci A. Purath MD, Neurology

The CHOICE is OURS
Bonnie Groessl

FIVE KEYS TO
HEALTH, HAPPINESS & ABUNDANCE

BALBOA PRESS
A DIVISION OF HAY HOUSE

Copyright © 2011 Bonnie Groessl

All rights reserved. No part of this book may be used or reproduced by any means, graphic, electronic, or mechanical, including photocopying, recording, taping or by any information storage retrieval system without the written permission of the publisher except in the case of brief quotations embodied in critical articles and reviews.

Balboa Press books may be ordered through booksellers or by contacting:

Balboa Press
A Division of Hay House
1663 Liberty Drive
Bloomington, IN 47403
www.balboapress.com
1-(877) 407-4847

Because of the dynamic nature of the Internet, any web addresses or links contained in this book may have changed since publication and may no longer be valid. The views expressed in this work are solely those of the author and do not necessarily reflect the views of the publisher, and the publisher hereby disclaims any responsibility for them.

The author of this book does not dispense medical advice or prescribe the use of any technique as a form of treatment for physical, emotional, or medical problems without the advice of a physician, either directly or indirectly. The intent of the author is only to offer information of a general nature to help you in your quest for emotional and spiritual well-being. In the event you use any of the information in this book for yourself, which is your constitutional right, the author and the publisher assume no responsibility for your actions.

Any people depicted in stock imagery provided by Thinkstock are models, and such images are being used for illustrative purposes only. Certain stock imagery © Thinkstock.

ISBN: 978-1-4525-3616-3 (sc)
ISBN: 978-1-4525-3617-0 (e)

Library of Congress Control Number: 2011910963

Printed in the United States of America

Balboa Press rev. date: 7/26/2011

Dedication

To my wonderfully loving and supportive husband, Mike, and to the many teachers and life experiences that have made me who I am today.

Acknowledgements

I want to thank those who shared their stories with me so I could share them with you. I especially want to thank my husband, Mike, who helped me get this manuscript ready for editing and onto my publisher. Without his writing skills and expertise as an author, I would not have met my timelines. I'd like to thank Julie Rogers for sharing her editing expertise.

Contents

Dedication	v
Acknowledgements	vii
Introduction	xiii
• A Word of Caution	xiv
• Our Stories	xiv
First Key - It Begins With Energy	1
• The Law of Attraction	2
• Placebo Versus Nocebo	3
• Our Thoughts Create Our Lives	3
• Taking it Off the Radar Screen	5
• The Twelve-Inch Ruler	6
• Abundance Games	8
• We See What We Think About	9
• Listen to Your Emotions	10
• Balance Your Energy	11
• Bring Strong Emotions to Neutral – EFT	13
• Some EFT Tips	17
• EFT Example - Craving	18
• What's the Core Issue?	19
• Good Energy Around Us	19
• The Ripple Affect	21
• Summary and Suggestions	23
Second Key – The Power of Our Thoughts and Emotions	24
• The Outer World	26
• Laughter is Good for Us	27
• We Should All Daydream	28
• Stress is a Part of Life	29

- Two-Minute Relaxation Technique — 31
- Thoughts Become Things — 32
- Our Brain and the Subconscious Mind — 34
- Hypnosis Happens - More Than We Realize — 38
- Can You Imagine? — 40
- The Power of Imagery — 42
- Induce a State of Deep Relaxation for Hypnosis — 43
- Imagery Exercise: Evoke a Feeling — 44
- Imagery Exercise: The Secret Garden — 46
- Imagery Exercise: Take a Mini Mental Vacation — 47
- Self-Hypnosis: Weight Loss — 49
- Symptom Imagery — 53
- Imagery Exercise: Symptom Imagery — 54
- Affirmations Can Be Powerful — 56
- The Bridge in Our Brain — 60
- What Do I Subconsciously Believe? — 61
- Muscle Testing Yourself — 62
- Summary and Suggestions — 65

Third Key – We Have a Choice — 66

- What Do You Choose to See? — 67
- Notice the So-What Issues — 68
- Choose to Eat Well — 71
- The Importance of Water — 74
- Everything in Moderation — 74
- Vitamins are Good Insurance — 76
- Magnesium: The Relaxation Mineral — 78
- Omega-3 – Fish Oil — 79
- Vitamin D: The Sunshine Vitamin — 79
- Are You Sensitive to Foods? — 80
- Choose to Get Moving — 80
- Choose to Give Your Body Rest — 82
- Restful Sleep Guided Meditation — 84
- Choose Self-Acceptance — 86
- Choose to Know You Are Important — 86
- Attitude of Gratitude — 87
- Anger and Forgiveness — 89
- Imagery Exercise: Forgiveness — 91
- Imagery Exercise: The Setting Sun — 92

- Imagery Exercise: To Alleviate Physical Pain 94
- Summary and Suggestions 95

Fourth Key – Experience Every Moment As It Is 96
- Mindful Meditation 98
- Living in the Present 99
- Mindfulness Meditation Practice 100
- Mindful Eating Practice 101
- Incorporate Mindfulness into Your Life 102
- Practice in Meditation 103
- Summary and Suggestions 106

Fifth Key – It's All About Love 107
- Our Heart - Another Brain? 108
- Exercise: Taking in the Love 109
- Spirituality – We Are Not Alone 110
- We All Have Inner Guidance 112
- Imagery Exercise: Inner Wisdom 115
- Do You Believe in Angels? 116
- Prayer 119
- Praying Rain 120
- Journaling 122
- Benefit of a Daily Routine 124
- Summary and Suggestions 126

Conclusion 127
- Plan Your Daily Practice 127

About the Author 129

Resources 131
- Suggested Reading 131
- Useful Websites 132

References 135

Introduction

"The most astonishing thing about miracles is that they happen."
~ G. K. Chesterton, English author and mystery novelist (1874 - 1936)

Do you have the life you want? Are you joyful? Do you wake up every morning excited for a new day? If this isn't your reality as often as you'd like, then this book is for you.

Many people today are suffering. Whether it's physical or emotional pain, life-threatening illness, grief, loneliness, anxiety, sadness, insecurity or just feeling overwhelmed by life, there is suffering. We deserve to be happy and live the lives we want. Life is what it is, but suffering is optional.

In this book you will learn the keys to a life with better health, better relationships, more abundance and more happiness. You can open the door to the life you want. We all have that power within us; we just need to access it. For some people, happiness means getting their life back; for others, it's achieving new things or experiencing more joy in life. Whatever it is for you, you must believe you can have the life you want. Belief is probably the best gift you can give yourself. You deserve to have the life you want. You need to believe that!

We have all heard of miraculous recoveries, near-death experiences, and people who continued living and enjoying their lives despite terminal cancer diagnoses. A common thread is they exceeded expectations, resulting in a better outcome than many around them might have imagined. Anything is possible and miracles DO happen.

I have learned much from great teachers during my lifetime. My goal is to introduce you to some of these tools and ideas as you begin your journey toward the life you want. I also will provide some resources for further exploration. There is always another way to look at something, and I hope to provide some ideas and possibilities for you. My intention is not to provide you with a complete list, since there are many ways to achieve positive results. These methods are some of my favorites, and the ones I have found to be most effective.

A Word of Caution

This book is not intended to be a substitute for professional care, or a treatment for any mental or physical condition. Different things work for different people. Although these ideas and treatments have helped many people, everyone is different. Sometimes a method might stir up uncomfortable feelings, especially if you have a traumatic history. If this is the case, seeking professional help or even discussing it with a friend may help. Change the method in some way so it fits for you, or just move on. Be kind to yourself. Being nonjudgmental and not beating yourself up is extremely important. Often we are kinder to others than to ourselves.

My spiritual beliefs have been my saving grace, helping me through many life challenges. Many people find their spiritual connection in religion. Please note that I am writing from the perspective of my beliefs and do not mean to impose them onto you. I believe it's important for us to find love and support from faith, believing in something greater than ourselves. It is important to believe that we are loved and deserve the life we want. Values and beliefs are a personal choice.

Our Stories

Everyone has a story. These stories are what create our lives. What we learn from these stories make us who we are today. Like you, I have many stories, but there was one from which I learned my biggest lesson.

It was 2009 and things were really going along pretty well in my life. I was happily married (and still am), my kids were grown, and I was very busy in my private practice as a nurse practitioner. Looking back, perhaps I was a little bit too busy. My thoughts mostly centered on work and doing what I believed I had to do each day. I didn't have much time to play, do the fun things or just do nothing. But: life was good and I was happy. Then, in July of 2009, my life took a detour.

It was midnight and my husband, Mike, and I were driving the highway speed limit of 65 mph. As we approached a rural intersection, the driver of a large pick-up truck failed to stop at a stop sign and drove directly into our path. We didn't have time to swerve. To avoid hitting the truck at a 90-degree angle, Mike turned the wheel a bit to the left. Upon impact, my head hit the passenger-side window hard. Despite wearing our seat belts and our air bags deploying, I was knocked unconscious, remaining in a coma for about three days. It was a blessing that Mike remained fully awake after the accident because he was able to keep my airway open. Additional help arrived quickly, and an ambulance was on the scene in less than five minutes. The downside is that my husband remembers everything about the crash.

My friends and family members talked to me as I lay unconscious in my hospital bed. They held my hand, prayed and waited for signs that I was waking up. I believe I heard them talking to me, because as I regained consciousness a few days later, I knew we had been in an accident. Initially, I couldn't walk or feed myself. It's as if my brain couldn't remember how to perform these simple tasks. I had difficulty understanding conversations and felt like the world was in slow motion. I couldn't remember phone numbers, the name of the president, what day it was, or even where we lived. I had trouble recognizing words and images. However, I could remember my loved ones.

A friend started a CaringBridge website on my behalf. It helped distant family and friends stay posted on my progress, and many people sent me prayers and messages of good thoughts and love. Loved ones at the hospital read the notes posted on the site to me. Even though my brain didn't function well, I understood what they were reading.

Despite that early inability to walk, I quickly graduated from a wheelchair to a walker to walking with assistance. I had to relearn how to move my body and balance. I wasn't able to feed myself, but my husband tells me it wasn't long before I just grabbed the fork from him and tried. I wasn't very coordinated at first. I'm right-handed and my right side was not working well because the injury was mainly to the left side of my brain. Intensive physical, occupational and speech therapy began as soon as I regained consciousness. If I wasn't in therapy, I was sleeping, and vice versa. My brain needed to rest in order to heal.

I don't remember much of my ten-day hospitalization. I remember bits and pieces, and not many of them at that. I continued therapy for a few months and was lucky, as my memory and my abilities quickly returned.

With therapy, love, prayers, persistence and lots of help, my recovery was nothing short of miraculous. My homework consisted of "brain exercises" that I did several times a day. I even did simple math problems in my head and other brain training in the shower.

Looking back, I realize having the memory loss was a blessing. I couldn't comprehend how bad my situation was, and if I had, I know it would have been even more difficult for me. Losing your memory of traumatic period can be a very protective mechanism. I can remember everything leading up to the accident, so it is only a relatively short period of time that I can't recall. I think I would have been frustrated with myself had I realized how little I could do at first. I think the memory loss was the universe's way of caring for me. The feeling I had during my recovery was beyond the feeling of being loved and cared for by other people. It seemed as though I could feel the universe protecting me. It was a sense that something bigger than me or other people around me – I believe it was God and the angels – were providing comfort, security, hope and a sense of well-being. It is a feeling of peace I had never before experienced. I knew at that time that everything would work out.

Just six weeks after the crash, I took my driving test again and passed – a requirement for people with brain injuries. I felt well enough to return to my practice on a limited basis. Initially I only saw one patient a day and restricted my activities. My practice centers on teaching and counseling. I talk with patients and teach them simple tools they can use on their own to help them feel better. I believed this was an aspect of my practice that I could do safely. It took me a long time to type the notes from that very first patient. My spelling was atrocious, and making sense of what I wanted to say on paper was challenging. I knew this low level of work was good therapy for me and I wanted to get my brain completely back.

It took me at least a year to feel completely normal again. My brain continues to improve daily as I continue to challenge myself and create new pathways in my brain. Math still isn't my best subject, but I have gained so much understanding and insight along the way.

I really don't remember having any negative thoughts about the accident or my injuries. I was never upset with the kids who were driving the truck that night, and was thankful they were not hurt badly. I felt at peace during the healing process and therapy. For my entire adult life, I have struggled with patience and maybe that was my lesson here. I certainly had the opportunity to practice it! I had faith I would get my life back and things would be just as they were or even better. As I was recovering, I spent time imagining that I had already healed, feeling appreciation.

Today I am happier than ever. I am not working as hard in my private practice, which is a good thing. Things don't bother me as much. I am grateful for everything, and I mean everything. I often stop and see the simple things around me, recognize what I am doing or notice something happening, and I feel so blessed that I am here to enjoy my life in a whole new way. I am doing things I never dreamed I would be doing. I have always been a very positive person, but this is a new level. I believe anyone can have that feeling if they choose. There is a feeling of joy and excitement for each new day. Sometimes it takes a traumatic event to feel that peaceful, joyful emotion about every day, but it doesn't have to be that extreme.

I truly believe there is a reason I survived and got a second chance at life that night. I also believe there is a reason I recovered so well and so quickly. There is a reason for my peace and feeling of being totally cared for.

I practice meditation, and have for several years. In meditation, we can access that inner guidance we all have. If we are still enough, we can hear the answers to questions we ask. I asked why I survived and recovered so well. The answer that came to me was simple: I had to prove it could be done; not just for me, but to inspire and give hope to others.

There have been many lessons and blessings from my accident. The biggest blessing was experiencing the power of prayer, love and positive energy from so many people, as well as my own positive thoughts. I have always been mindful of the tremendous healing power within each of us, and now I have first-hand experience.

This is why I am so passionate about helping you have the life you want. Even if the odds are against you, you must believe you can have it. My recovery was nothing short of remarkable, and I am thankful every day for my life. I know I am not the only one to have experienced this type of healing. I have read countless stories of people who survived the odds against cancer, terrible accidents and other life-threatening events. I am honored to be among them.

I want this book to be a resource for you, to add tools to your toolbox and create the life you want.

Your Journey Begins...

First Key - It Begins With Energy

"Hard work is not the path to well-being. Feeling good is the path to well-being. You don't create through action; you create through vibration. And then, your vibration calls action from you."
- Abraham Hicks

Everything in the universe is made of energy, and all energy vibrates. Albert Einstein proved that when you come right down to it, everything in the universe is energy. The concept of the universal flow of energy is not a new one. The ancient Chinese called this flow *chi*; the ancient Hindus called it *prana*.

Current research on quantum physics reveals that we all came from energy. It is impossible for us to have come from cells like the ones from which we are made without energy being part of the equation. We had to begin somewhere. Often we see ourselves separate from other people, yet we are all one. We all began from energy. We have concluded the entire universe is made up of thinking (intelligent) "non-stuff" (particles or waves) with no matter or mass. This non-stuff is associated with thought.

Quantum physics is a science that studies and attempts to explain how everything in our world comes into existence. It begins with the physical aspect of the events, conditions and circumstances of everything in the universe, and breaks everything down into its most basic form, attempting to discover the source from which everything is derived. Quantum physics, spirituality, thoughts, emotions, and success or lack of success, are closely interconnected. In the early 1900s, Einstein was one of the founders of quantum theory, which proved that all things broken down to their most basic form consist of the same stuff, pure energy. This changed how we view the workings of the universe. Everything – be it nature, sound, color, oxygen, thoughts, emotions, the wind, your chair, house, car, dog, or physical body, the stars, your ability to see, hear, smell and so on – exists only because of this very same energy.

Energy equals vibration. We know we have different frequencies of energy, or vibration. We also know this frequency depends on our own thoughts, our inner mental and feeling world. If, for example, we feel inadequate and short-changed by life itself, we vibrate at a different frequency than if we feel abundant, confident and accept ourselves completely. Negative inner dialogue then controls our life, since it manifests on the material level with negative results. No matter how much we seek happiness or aim for success in anything, it remains out of reach, leaving behind frustration. It's easy to forget that our inner thoughts and feelings ultimately lead us toward or away from our goals and dreams.

It comes down to this: we are beings made up of energy. That energy creates vibration when we think and feel. We get what we vibrate; our thoughts and feelings create our vibrations. If you don't like what you're experiencing, it's helpful to change your vibration – change what you're thinking and feeling. Our beliefs, expectations, stories – all of our life experiences – contribute to our overall vibration.

The Law of Attraction

"Like attracts like" is the simple definition of the Law of Attraction. The Universal Law of Attraction is the most powerful force in the universe. It is a simple concept but sometimes difficult to put into practice on a regular basis.

Remember, we are beings made up of energy, and our thoughts and feelings create vibration. We get what matches our vibration. We all focus on what we don't want at times. The key is to avoid staying there, to notice we are off course and then return our focus to what we want, and feel as though we're already there.

The Law of Attraction simply says that you attract into your life whatever you think about and what you vibrate, which includes your feelings. Your dominant thoughts will find a way to manifest. Dominant is the operative word here. This universal law is working in your life right now, whether you are aware of it or not. You are attracting people, situations, jobs and much more into your life. Once you are aware of this law and how it works, you can start to use it to deliberately attract what you want into your life.

This is not New Age stuff; the earliest written record of this principle dates back to *The Emerald Tablet* in about 3000 B.C. The ancient text of the *Tabula Smaragdina (The Emerald Tablet)*, after being translated into Latin as <u>Secretum Secretorum</u> *(The Secret of Secrets)*, became prominent in Western spirituality. The Law of Attraction is related to this old, esoteric document that begins with the words, "as above, so below." In this saying, "above" represents the outer world, and "below" represents our inner world – our thoughts, emotions and beliefs.

Placebo Versus Nocebo

Medicine also uses the principle of the Law of Attraction, which is similar to the placebo effect. Many of us have heard the term "placebo effect." Research uses this technique, especially when testing the effectiveness of drugs. If a patient receives sugar pills and has the same result as actual medication, it is called a placebo effect. The individual believes the pills they are receiving are actual medicine and will help their symptoms, so it does. Our thoughts sometimes create a placebo effect.

Not as many people have heard about the "nocebo effect," which is just as powerful. The nocebo effect is the opposite of the placebo effect in that it produces a negative reaction. This can occur if someone suffers from a chronic illness or some type of pain, and their health-care provider tells them there is nothing that can be done and they must learn to cope. Whether there is a treatment or not, and whether that person can improve or not, the nocebo effect means they probably won't improve because they received that message.

The nocebo effect can be debilitating. "Judy" has had daily headaches since the age of sixteen. She is now in her fifties. When asked what happened in her life when the headaches began as a teen, she says she hit her head. The doctor who examined her told her that because she hit her head really hard, she would have a headache for the rest of her life. And she has.

Our Thoughts Create Our Lives

Our thoughts become things. What do you think about? The life you lead reveals the answer. If you are happy and successful, you think thoughts of happiness and success. If you are wading through an endless stream of problems and are unhappy in life, your thoughts may be filled with doubt, failure, anger, helplessness, fear and pain.

A positive mind expects happiness, joy and blessings. If you stay positive and think joyful, uplifting thoughts, your whole being will broadcast happiness and success. It has been proven that even health is affected in a beneficial way when your thoughts stay positive. Studies show that people who consciously make an effort to stay positive have a much more successful life and get through difficult times easier than negative people. Now, it's OK to feel worry, fear or doubt sometimes. Just don't stay there! You can't have positive thoughts 100 percent of the time. Your feelings should be acknowledged and honored, then return to feeling good and focusing on more positive thoughts.

What causes the feelings of worry, doubt and fear? Sometimes it's a limiting belief or some form of resistance. This keeps us stuck and holds us back from having the life we want. It's not possible to go from despair to happiness all in one big jump. Inspirational speakers and best-selling authors Esther and Jerry Hicks, of Abraham-Hicks Publications (www.abraham-hicks.com) and available through Hay House Inc., promote the concept of simply reaching for the feeling of relief, enjoying that, and then reaching again for relief.

I use the analogy of climbing a ladder. We don't just jump to the top rung; we climb one step at a time. It's important to be nonjudgmental the entire way. If we think we are not going fast enough or doing it correctly, we will struggle. The harder we try, the more we struggle, the less we achieve.

Be gentle with yourself. Self-criticism is negative thinking. Would you scold a child or someone you cared about if they were climbing the ladder too slowly? Of course you wouldn't. You would encourage them with compassion and love. We often are much kinder to others than we are to ourselves.

Whatever we focus on the most is what will be most attracted to our life. At first glance, it would seem that since we all think about being healthy, having enough money and fulfilling lives, we'd have that. That's only true if we believe we already have those things we desire. The truth is that most people focus on NOT having those things.

If thoughts of health, wealth and happiness dominate your life, you must realize you really may be focusing more on what you don't have. That's not what you want. If you wish for those things and don't have the feeling that you already have them, you are coming from a place of lack, and you will get more of the same.

Let's use the example of money. Wishing for more money to pay the bills or afford a trip only brings you more debt. It would better serve you to change your thoughts a bit. Think about the bills being paid and how good that feels. Give gratitude for having the resources to pay your bills this month. Imagine what it feels like to enjoy a vacation, dining out, or buying something without paying attention to the price. Let the feeling of abundance dominate your thoughts. I am not saying to foolishly spend money you don't have, but feel good about what you do have, and let that be the source of abundant thinking. You will then be attracting the money you want.

Taking it Off the Radar Screen

Abundance can be many things. We can imagine having abundant health, relationships and general happiness. We pretend we're already there and it feels good.

I always say that if you can't have positive thoughts about something, the next best thing is to not think about it at all. Just take it off the radar screen. The more you put your attention on what you don't want, the more you attract it and the more you experience it. The only way to attract what you desire in life is to allow yourself to imagine what it feels like to have what you want, to allow yourself to believe that you will have it, that you deserve it, and focus on those positive feelings and beliefs on a consistent basis.

Removing negative thoughts from the radar screen is powerful. "Charles" was in his thirties, recently married and enjoying his life. Then, he developed a rare form of cancer with few or no treatment options available. The doctors gave Charles less than two years to live. There was only one other person with this type of cancer who survived longer than five years. At first Charles was devastated, but then he chose to deal with it his own way. He took his prognosis off the radar screen, paid no attention to it. With no good treatment options anyway, he continued to live his life as though the cancer didn't exist. He never talked about it and didn't want to know his test results. He lived life the way he wanted and didn't pay any attention to the "c" word. His friends seldom, if ever, brought it up. He worked, planted his gardens, traveled and simply enjoyed life as he always had, and he felt good. That was nine years ago and he still feels good. He does not look or feel like someone with cancer. I don't know his test results or what his scans show, but what does it matter? He is living his life to the fullest.

Miracles do happen. I truly believe that not focusing his attention on the cancer made a difference for Charles. He focused on what he wanted, rather than what he didn't want.

The Law of Attraction works for everything. It doesn't decide if we deserve something or not. We are all deserving of the life we want. We can use this principle if we are struggling with a relationship, job, health issue or whatever the case may be. It's as simple as living as though we already have the life we want, and feeling thankful.

I realize it's hard to imagine your life being what you want if it's not there yet. However, leveraging your power of imagination is essential to moving toward that ideal life. If you can't imagine it, it can't happen.

Do you know what you want? Just like a map, you have a destination and a path to get there.

If we don't know where we are going, how will we know when we are there? Sometimes we don't take the time to think about this. We are busy going to work, getting the kids to soccer, taking care of the house and paying bills. I often ask the "miracle" question: If a miracle happens tonight while you are asleep, and tomorrow morning the world as you know it is the way you want it – your perfect dream life – what would that look like? You may want to take some quiet time and ponder this for a while. Get a pen and paper and write down your thoughts. This could be your wish list.

Don't misunderstand me. The Law of Attraction is not magic. We don't manifest material goods or personal success simply by thinking about them. However, the universe provides us with what we need; the people, methods and opportunities to help us achieve what we want. Hard work may be a part of the equation or maybe not. The key is for us to see the opportunities and make the most of them.

The Twelve-Inch Ruler

One of the best resources I have found is Esther and Jerry Hicks' Teachings of Abraham. In one of their talks, they use the analogy about two ends of a stick. I draw a line at the six-inch marker of a twelve-inch ruler and often use this to make the same point. At one end of the ruler, the zero mark represents what we don't want. The other end of the ruler, the twelve-inch mark, is what we do want. We want to be between the six-inch mark and the twelve-inch mark as often as possible. Most of the time, we're either on one side of that six-inch mark or the other. We're either closer to what we want (the twelve-inch mark) or closer to what we don't want (the zero mark). It's human nature to go back and forth, feeling differently from time to time. The goal is to be in the upper half, the six- to twelve-inch range, most of the time, especially as we are thinking of something we want.

So, think carefully. Where are you are on a ruler at any given point in time as you think about something?

For example, imagine you are struggling with a relationship issue. Are you are thinking: "Oh, I will never find anyone. I am not good enough, thin enough; my perfect soul mate doesn't exist. I will be single all my life. Why does everyone have a partner except me?" If you are thinking that way, you're probably within the zero- to six-inch range. You are closer to what you don't want. That's the energy you're vibrating.

We get what we expect. We attract like vibrations, and we are sending out a vibration of scarcity when we're at the lower end of the ruler.

Do you look at lessons you learned from former dates – what you want and don't want? Do you enjoy spending time alone? Do you fantasize about how it feels to be in a good relationship? Do you enjoy that good, loved feeling, even though you're not quite there? Are you confident that somehow things will be fine and eventually work out? If so, you're probably closer to the twelve-inch end of the ruler. You're more toward what you want.

Notice how much of the time you are heading in the right direction, toward what you want, and how much of the time you are not. Where are you most of the time?

"Rhonda" was in a lonely marriage, devoting most of her time and attention to her kids and work since her marriage was not in a place where she felt good. In spare moments throughout the day, she would fantasize about being in a loving, happy relationship. She didn't imagine what her partner would be like, but rather, how she would feel. Daydreaming about what she wanted gave her a good feeling that was lacking in her marriage. She believed she needed to stay married for the children, and thought perhaps she was expecting too much. After all, there was no physical abuse. She was unhappy and lonely, but her children were her love. Then one day, after twenty years, the marriage ended. Within a couple of months, she found the relationship about which she had been dreaming. She wasn't actively looking; in fact, it was the furthest thing from her mind. But "he" found her. Today, Rhonda and her new husband are happily married and everything has worked out for her and her kids. She has everything she dreamed of in terms of a relationship. Rhonda spent time daydreaming about what she wanted, and felt as though she was already there. She spent more time on the upper half (twelve-inch mark) of the ruler.

When you think back on life, doesn't everything eventually work out? One way or another, things just do. Sometimes we experience difficult situations along the way – challenges, struggles, and detours in life – but things always seem to end up working out. Although we may not see it at the time, very often it's for the best, and in the end, we're OK.

When we think about or focus on something, that's what we see, and in turn, it's what we experience. If our vibration is high, we will get things in our lives of equal vibration. If our vibration is low – not feeling worthy, feeling lacking, not feeling good about ourselves, feeling sad or fearful – we still get the things in our vibration, but they aren't what we want.

Abundance Games

There are ways to increase that vibration regarding abundance. Here are a few:

First, think positively about abundance. One of the games my husband and I play is the abundance game. We simply notice all the abundance in our lives, whether it's finding a penny or nickel on the floor or sidewalk, receiving an unexpected gift, or just experiencing something good we didn't expect. Sometimes when we are at a restaurant and our order is wrong, we'll receive an extra side dish or dessert to make up for the mistake. In our little game, we call that abundance and we take note of it. For a while, we actually wrote those things down.

This is a good practice to start, especially when you begin to look at abundance differently. When you notice it, write it down. Keep a list. It doesn't have to be anything big, and it doesn't have to be monetary. It can just be any little surprise, like finding a parking spot close to the entrance of a store. Sometimes even surprises that initially seem negative may turn out to be positive. Recognize that as abundance.

You will be amazed at how many things happen in a typical day that gives us cause to say, "Abundance!" In general, people don't recognize the little abundances that occur every day, and that's a missed opportunity for gratitude.

We usually notice the negative things. That makes the negative things our dominant feeling, and that doesn't help our energy, vibration, feelings or achievements.

"The Lottery Game" is another abundance game we play. We look at what the jackpot is for the lottery and pretend we have won. We may not even buy a ticket, just look at the amount. Then we talk about how we would use the money. We make imaginary decisions, like who would help us with the legal issues, whom we would give money to and what charities we would support. We dream about what we would buy or do for ourselves. You get the picture. The goal is to feel good doing this and not just make a joke of it (but it is fun). My husband and I already have made many decisions for when we win the lottery. Things don't always come in the package you expect them to. We often say that surviving the car accident and having the life we have is like winning the lottery for us.

Develop your own games about abundance and see what happens. Remember, abundance relates to everything, it's not just money. Abundance can be good health, a good relationship, fun with friends, etc. So when you have little things that please you or surprise you throughout the day, acknowledge that abundance in your life. I would bet that the more abundance you look for, the more abundance you will see and thus the more abundance you will actually receive.

We See What We Think About

When someone wants to be pregnant or is thinking about being pregnant, they suddenly see every other pregnant woman in town. They never realized there were so many women having babies! We see what is in our awareness. Because they are focusing on a baby or getting pregnant, that's what they see. In reality, there were just as many pregnant women before, but they didn't notice them.

A few years ago, I bought a new car. I don't know much about cars. To me, it was just a green car. As I'm driving down the street with my little green car, I suddenly notice all the other green cars on the road. Those cars were always there, but I didn't notice them because I wasn't thinking about a green car until I had one. I focused on my green car, so that's what I saw.

I believe it's very true that whatever you focus your attention on gets bigger, whether it's your dreams or your fears.

Now, it's difficult not to think about the negative things going on in our lives because that's what's in our face. That's our experience. It's a challenge to look at things in a different way. There's always more than one way to perceive something. We all know people who have a lot of drama in their lives. I'm not saying that people bring bad things to themselves intentionally, or even consciously. The drama may be in their lives because of damaging subconscious thoughts or feelings. This lowers their vibration, and thus attracts like-vibration events.

"Melanie" was irritated that someone wasn't helping her with a project. She was grumbling to herself and not in a very good mood. Everything seemed to go wrong with the project: electric cords became unplugged; pieces were missing and she had to stop and find them; she even tripped and skinned her knee. It was one thing after the other. Then, realizing her vibration was contributing to the situation, she decided to change her attitude and not feel irritated anymore. She chose to feel thankful that she had this project, and things began working better.

Has that ever happened to you?

Sometimes, I think we experience things because there are things we need to learn. Oftentimes we can learn a lesson even from a bad experience, and be better for it. We don't always know what that lesson is at the time. Sometimes it becomes obvious only years later. Then we can say, "Ah, that's why that happened." It's like a domino effect. If that one thing wouldn't have happened, the next thing wouldn't have happened, and the next, and the next. I think that as adults, we sometimes forget that life is a journey and there are going to be detours, pit stops and potholes in the road.

I believe in the old saying that there are no accidents. I believe things happen for a reason. This has helped me understand and deal with life's challenges along the way. I've been on detours myself. Life is a journey, not just a destination. We do the best with what we have.

I think that even when people do terrible things, sometimes they are really doing the best they can with what they have. Granted, their self-esteem, love, happiness, etc., is probably low. They are empty, but they are still doing their best. Believing this helps me stay positive and handle the roadblocks and detours I encounter on my journey.

Listen to Your Emotions

Feelings and emotions tell us what we are thinking about at a subconscious level. Be aware of how much of the time you feel good and how much of the time you don't. Take a day to create an inventory and give yourself a percentage of time you felt good versus not so good. What percent of the time do you feel confident, hopeful and happy? How much of the time do you feel like there is always enough and that things always work out? Then take inventory of the percentage of time you have thoughts such as you're not good enough, there isn't enough money, or you find yourself thinking more about what's not going well. Your feelings and emotions will tell you a lot about what you are thinking on a subconscious level. How do you feel most of the time? Notice how much of the time you head in the right direction, toward what you want, and how much of the time you don't. Also, notice if there are beliefs that keep you stuck. It could be a belief you have from years ago, maybe even as a child. Perhaps it's a belief that you don't deserve something or that you're not good enough.

Do you want something you don't currently have? It's easy to focus on what we don't have because it's in our life every day. Whether it is a romantic relationship, more money or anything else that is lacking ... we probably think about it a lot. We can shift our thoughts, and more importantly our feelings, to what we do want and engage the Law of Attraction to help manifest our desires.

We need to be a vibrational match to what we want so it can manifest in our lives. Have you ever heard the expression, "She's wearing rose-colored glasses"? Well, that's not a bad idea! We notice, see and experience what we think about. Thoughts and feelings create our vibration. In difficult times, I think some of us wear dark, cloudy glasses rather than rose-colored ones. It's how we see the world. That becomes our vibration, and thus also what we attract.

Balance Your Energy

Crossing different parts of our body is good for our energy flow. Our brain functions better when the right and left hemispheres work in tandem. From the time we are babies, crawling across the carpet, we develop our brains by using opposite arms and legs to stimulate the left and right hemispheres at the same time. As adults, one way we can increase our functioning on all levels is by taking regular walks, especially if we swing our arms back and forth across our body. Walking in this manner encourages the left and right hemispheres to communicate with each other.

When we put one foot forward, we control it with the opposite hemisphere of the brain. The left hemisphere controls the right side of our body, and vice versa. If we swing our arms across our body while walking, we encourage the hemispheres of the brain to work in synchronized cooperation. It also improves our energy. These crossover patterns improve coordination, breathing, balance, hearing, vision and overall health. We reinforce these functions by crossing our body, such as swinging our arms while we walk.

Sitting at a computer all day or just dealing with the stresses of everyday life can hinder communication between the hemispheres of our brain as well as create barriers that prevent our energy from crossing. We refer to this issue as our brain and energy being homolateral. We can correct this by simply marching in place or crossing our arms over our body while walking, as mentioned previously. We can also do this by sitting in a chair, twisting our upper torso slightly to bring our right hand to our left knee and our left hand to our right knee.

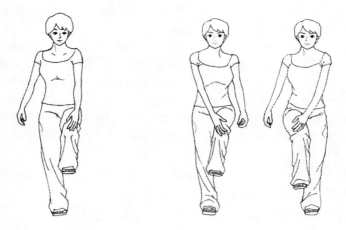

If you find yourself struggling to think clearly or have no energy, you might feel better by doing a variation on this exercise. First, march without crossing. To do this, start by moving your right arm with your right leg, and the left arm with the left leg. This movement may feel smooth to you, and if it does, it could mean you are more homolateral. In other words, your energy and the hemispheres of your brain are not crossing. Next, begin marching with your arms swinging across your body. Crossing right to left and left to right. This may feel a little awkward at first.

If you repeat the process of going back and forth between not crossing your body and then crossing your body while marching, pretty soon the crossing pattern will begin to feel the more comfortable option. Your energy should be crossing better, too. You can do this marching pattern back and forth between same side (right to right and left to left) and then switch into the crossing process, swinging your arms across your body or actually touching your right hand to the left leg and vice versa several times. It's a good idea to march each way at least ten steps before switching. You always want to end on a good note, so end with marching while swinging your arms across your body.

Perform this exercise until you feel more comfortable crossing your arms than allowing them to swing straight. This tells you that your energy and your brain are crossing more than when you started, and you should begin feeling better. When our energy and our brains are crossing, it reduces the effects of stress and improves our emotions, memory, balance and mental clarity. It even increases our physical energy. Doing this exercise is a great way to start the day, or anytime you feel stressed or just a little off.

Modify this technique to fit your physical ability. I have done this in groups where people are not able to stand or march. I had people in a Parkinson's support group do this while sitting in wheelchairs. They just used their arms to cross their bodies, gently tapping or getting close to their knees. They enjoyed the benefit of energy and well-being, even though they couldn't march. Remember, any technique is as much about your intention as the technique itself.

Additional Resources:

Donna Eden teaches people how to work with the body's energy systems to reclaim their health and natural vitality. For more information, visit www.innersource.net.

Brain Gym® International is a nonprofit organization committed to the principle that intentional movement is the door to optimal living and learning. For more information, go to www.braingym.org.

Bring Strong Emotions to Neutral – EFT

How do you get your strong emotions and feelings to settle down so you feel calmer? As human beings, we have many intense emotions. Bliss and joy are intense emotions we want to enjoy and bask in for a while because they feel good. That raises our vibration. However, what about the emotions that don't make us feel good, like craving a chocolate chip cookie, anxiety, anger, or sadness?

Relaxation techniques and breathing exercises are helpful, of course, but another great tool that I use for myself and in my practice is the EFT (Emotional Freedom Technique). EFT is easy to learn and helps calm those strong feelings. This technique also helps release limiting beliefs in the subconscious mind.

EFT is a form of meridian tapping and psychological acupuncture. Because we can't separate the mind from the body, emotional health is essential to our physical health and well-being. You can use EFT for just about anything. EFT works similarly to acupuncture, but you don't use any needles. The meridians are the channels through which *chi* (energy) flows to nourish and energize our body. You just tap – a form of acupressure – on different acupuncture/acupressure points located on meridians as you focus on a feeling. This is a bilateral system, so you can tap on either side or alternate, whatever is comfortable. Your body likely will just do what's right for you, so go with what feels the most natural. I know it may seem a bit different at first, but it really works.

This technique is useful in taking whatever strong emotion you are in and bringing it to a neutral place. It doesn't matter what it is. It could be a craving for a chocolate chip cookie, or it could be fear, anxiety or sadness. When you tap on these different points, focusing on that feeling, you move the energy and bring that strong feeling to a neutral place. Neutral is better than being in the intense emotion. This combination of tapping on acupuncture/acupressure points while focusing on an emotion helps clear the beliefs that keep us stuck.

EFT is something you can do for yourself, or a practitioner can help get you started by dealing with some of the big issues and teaching you the techniques.

The process starts with identifying the problem and adding an affirmation: "Even though I have this problem _____," followed by a positive statement such as, "I completely accept myself anyway." In the process of performing EFT, this is called the set-up statement. Some people ask me if identifying what they don't want lowers their vibration. They wonder if that is going against the Law of Attraction. I have found that it's important to identify the problem so you have a starting point, and then follow it up with something positive. Remember, it's an energy thing. Identifying the problem and saying something positive to follow it up while tapping provides a psychological reversal of the energy. When we voice positive affirmations, even if we are talking about the problem, it works to clear our emotional block.

To go through the basic technique of how to do meridian tapping, or EFT in this case, refer to the following illustration.

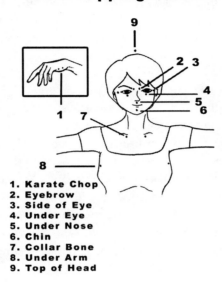

Sometimes people have a hard time saying something positive about themselves. Use whatever statement works for you. I like to add the word "anyway," as I find this makes it easier to voice a positive statement, especially if there are issues with self-acceptance.

I like using EFT as it is a simple recipe of tapping that works on just about everything. Some of the other meridian tapping techniques can be a bit complicated and overwhelming to people when they first begin. Healthcare providers worldwide use EFT. My first EFT workshop was with Carol Look (carollookeft.com). More and more research on this technique is available, and one day it may become part of mainstream medicine. There is a lot of information available on the internet to help people do this at home. The high success rate of EFT has rapidly spread through the medical community. Some of the best resources I have found are:

Information and products: www.thetappingsolution.com
Membership site: www.tappinginsidersclub.com/members
Information, products, and research: www.eftuniverse.com

The meridian/EFT system is a bilateral system, so you can use either hand or you can switch back and forth to tap. It's best to tap with the pads of two or three fingers on the karate chop point (see photo), which is the side of the hand, along with a series of points on our face and body.

The most important part of EFT is the set-up statement. Always begin with one. Identify what your issue is and then follow it with a positive statement. "Even though I have this problem _____, I completely accept myself anyway."

As an example, let's say we are working on anxiety. We say something like, "Even though I am so anxious, I completely accept myself anyway." We repeat this set-up statement three times while tapping on the karate chop point with the pads of our fingers, and then we begin tapping on the other points. As you tap on the other points, focus on the problem. You can add words as you are tapping on the other points. You could use the same word or phrase, like "I feel so anxious" or just say "anxiety" while tapping on each point. You still will receive benefit, whether you say the same word or phrase aloud or if you just say it to yourself. However, remember that the words are not as important as focusing on the feeling.

Here are the points again:
1. **Karate chop point** – fleshy outside edge of your hand
2. **Eyebrow point** – the point where the eyebrow begins, close to the curve of the nose
3. **Side of the eye point** - on the bone at the outside of the eye
4. **Under-eye point** - on top of the bone directly under the eye
5. **Under-nose point** - below the nose and above the top lip
6. **Chin point** - the natural crease in the chin below the bottom lip, where a dimple would be
7. **Collarbone point (or K-27)** – The collarbone is the hard, boney spot at the base of the neck. Move down one inch and find the soft spot just under your collarbone, this is the K-27 point.
8. **Under-arm point** – under the arm, midway down the torso (where the bra line is for women)

9. **Top of the head** – in a little circle at the top of your head (there are lots of acupuncture points that meet at the top of your head)

The most important part of the process is saying the set-up statement while tapping on the karate chop point. I have had one person in the past five years tell me the tapping didn't work. I asked him to show me how he did it, and he forgot to say the set-up statement while doing the karate chop.

Some EFT Tips

I usually have people tap at the K-27 spot, which is the soft spot just under the collarbone. We also want to catch as many of the acupuncture points that meet near the top of your head as we can, so I usually suggest tapping in a little circle at the top of the head. You don't have to tap very hard; be gentle. I would tap three to five times on each point, using the pads of three fingers so that you're sure to hit the right spot. (If you use just one finger, you must be exactly on the point or you will miss it.) However, the EFT process is forgiving. If you don't hit the spot just right, it still will work. The brain doesn't know the difference between real and imaginary. Just imagining the process is useful as well. You can stimulate these points in a number of different ways. You don't have to tap to stimulate the acupuncture point. It can be a light touch, too, if you have pain issues. You also can just imagine the spot and take a deep breath.

When I was recovering from my brain injury, the side of the eye area on the right side was extremely tender for many months. It was painful to tap there, so I just lightly touched that point and tapped in the rest of the places.

Modify any technique for your comfort or for your situation. The process doesn't matter as much as the intention you have when you are doing it.

When I do this work with patients in the office, I usually ask them to draw on an intense emotion. This is the best way to show them the effectiveness of this technique. I ask them to remember something that happened that really bothered them. If we are working on smoking cessation or weight loss, I have them focus on the craving for a cigarette or for food they can't resist. Sometimes I ask people to bring the food or cigarettes with them, so they can have the smell or feel, to help them really get into the craving. Then we do the tapping process. Generally, it doesn't take long for the intensity of their craving, desire or emotion to subside.

When using EFT or meridian tapping, remove your glasses and watches. Glasses can get in the way of your tapping points, and watches create electrical interference with the energy of EFT.

You may use the entire technique or you may find one particular spot that is especially helpful in reducing your intense emotion. Often it is that spot just below the collarbone, the K-27 point. Always use the karate chop and say the set-up statement. When I start a new round of tapping, I always begin with the set-up statement. I usually say it three times, as there is something special about the number three, but you can say it more than that. Then go into the tapping sequence. Sometimes people just need the set-up statement and tapping on the karate chop point, and that is enough to help them.

Do whatever works for you. I want everything in this book to be do-able in your life.

EFT Example - Craving

So let's use the example of craving a chocolate chip cookie. (As you try this, you can substitute the chocolate chip cookie for anything you want to work on.) Think of all the things you really like about that chocolate chip cookie. Maybe it's the chocolate taste, the sweetness, the aroma, or its texture, its chewiness. Increase your desire by imagining its taste and how it feels in your mouth as you chew. Rate it on a scale of zero to ten. The higher the number the better, as we want to work with an intense feeling. A set-up statement could be, "Even though I really want that chocolate chip cookie, I completely accept myself anyway." Say the set-up statement three times while tapping on the karate chop point. Then, while you are focusing on how much you want that cookie, begin tapping on the other points (see image) and repeat, "I really want that cookie." You can say the same statement, as the feeling is what's important. You can add other phrases or words such as, "It smells good," "I can almost taste it," or "I love that chocolate; it just melts in my mouth." Tap on the points with each phrase. Do two to three rounds of tapping in this manner and then stop.

How do you feel? How badly do you want the cookie? Check in, give it a number if you like, and see if the desire came down. You can repeat this sequence as often as necessary. When tapping on the other points, I've been successful in eliminating the target problem, even if my statements focus only on what I don't want or I repeat the same words over and over, like "I really want that chocolate chip cookie."

What's the Core Issue?

If your number isn't moving, there may be something else underneath the desire. When you begin EFT, it's important to identify the root cause of your particular issue. Do some exploration first. Ask yourself questions like the ones below:

- How long have I had this problem, and what was going on in my life when it started?
- Am I frustrated that I haven't had success with what I have tried before? If you are frustrated or feel like a failure, work on that first.
- If I didn't focus on this problem, who would I be and how would I feel?
- What's the benefit of keeping this?
- What will change if I let go of this problem?
- If this problem represents an emotion, what emotion is it (fear, anger, etc.)

"Christine" had been struggling with anger issues for a long time. She had a short fuse and would stay angry about things for a long time. She discovered many things in her adult life triggered her past experiences as a child. She held onto the resentment and anger from the past. Her intense emotion was interfering with her relationships, work and personal life. After using EFT, she was better able to set boundaries and not fly off the handle. She found it easier to let things go and accept others as they were. She was no longer triggering those childhood memories as she had been for so many years.

Good Energy Around Us

It's important to surround yourself with good energy. We have all experienced walking into a room and getting a bad feeling or a bad vibe. We get a very different feeling walking into a room surrounded by positive energy. The atmosphere radiates happiness, and we feel good just being there.

We all know people who always seem upbeat, happy and perky. We feel good just being around them. They have this positive energy; they enjoy life. They vibrate at a higher frequency than someone who isn't in that happy, positive place. When we're around negative people, they seem to sap all our energy. We may enter the interaction feeling upbeat, but after spending some time with these people, we feel down, weak, even tired. When we don't feel good, when we feel sad, angry, fearful or anxious, we're vibrating at a lower frequency. That feeling is contagious and soon others begin to feel that way, too. It's partly because like attracts like in terms of energy.

Energy is also contagious. It's important to surround yourself with the people who make you feel good and share that good energy. I am not saying you have to break ties with people who don't make you feel good; just don't spend a lot of time with them. Choose to spend time with the people who make you feel good. You can do the same for them by being feeling good, being happy and thinking positively.

People will want to be around you if you are feeling good. They can feel your vibration even though they may not know what that is. Aren't there people you know and it just feels good to be around them? People notice your energy and you notice theirs. Surround yourself with good people as often as possible.

You also can protect yourself from those "energy-sucking vampires" by just setting the intention that you're not going to absorb their negative energy. It's their choice to feel a particular way. You don't have to join them. Sometimes imagining a white light surrounding you, like a protective covering, is helpful.

Our main energy centers, called *chakras*, are along the center of our body. *Chakras* are energy centers based on India's ancient medical tradition known as *Ayurveda*. These spinning, wheel-like centers start at the base of your spine and end above your head. There are seven main *chakras* (see image). Each has a special quality that contributes to your overall constitution, health and consciousness. They take in energy from your surroundings and the universe. To give protection to these energy centers, imagine a huge zipper that starts at the base of your spine (or groin area) and goes all the way up your body to the top of your head. Then imagine zipping the zipper, protecting you from negative energy.

I know this may seem strange, but it really works.

"Joyce" was having a problem with a friend. She felt depressed and fatigued after spending time with her, but did not want to avoid her. I taught her the zipper technique, how to protect her *chakras* from taking in negative energy, and she found a big difference. She could spend time with her friend and not feel depleted afterwards.

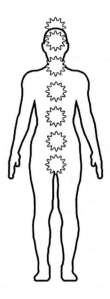

Read more about *chakras* at www.chakraenergy.com.

The Ripple Affect

Some people see the glass half empty. We all know people like that; perhaps you are like that from time to time. It's OK to have those feelings and that lower vibration sometimes. It's human nature to have anger, anxiety, frustration and worry. Just don't live there; don't let that be your dominant vibration and make that into who you are. Everybody will have times when their vibration is lower. Every emotion is simply an emotion. It's not necessarily good or bad, it's just an emotion. However, some emotions leave us not feeling good, and we don't want to be there too much of the time.

It's to our advantage to spend time with people who make us feel good. Perhaps somebody you live with has a "glass half-empty" perception of life and it brings you down. Depending on your relationship, you may want to say something to that person or get some help. Find a third party, even a counselor or a therapist, who will talk with both of you. It's better for both of you to be in a good place. If you shift your energy so that you're in a higher vibration and feeling better, as though the glass is half full, everything in your surroundings will change, including your partner. You will see them differently. Remember, we see what we focus on. You may have a better relationship with that person, and they may be more positive because the good energy you have is contagious.

"Cynthia's" relationship with her husband was less than perfect lately. He was unhappy with his job and didn't want to do anything when he got home after work. He just wanted to be alone. Yet, Cynthia wanted to go for a bike ride or have a conversation. She was frustrated and unhappy that he didn't want to engage in activities with her. She missed the husband she had fallen in love with. She decided to stop asking him to do things. She called friends and enjoyed being alone as well. As a result, she was happier and shifted her energy. In a couple of weeks, her husband was asking her if she wanted to go for a walk or talk about something, even go out to dinner. She couldn't change him, but when she changed herself, he changed, too.

Energy goes both ways, so you can influence your partner just by being in a better place. You can bring other people up and not allow them to bring you down.

We are all a part of a ripple every day in the things we say and do… random acts of kindness, sharing a smile, or just acknowledging someone. When my husband and I go to a restaurant, we always interact with the wait staff. We ask them their story, where they are from, etc. We have had many interesting conversations and met many wonderful people this way.

I encourage you to be aware of your actions and notice what type of a ripple you are sending out. We all affect each other's lives every day. Sometimes we don't even know we are doing it. We may be affecting someone we pass on the street.

I heard someone say that anyone can be a healer, whether they are a health-care provider or they work in a tollbooth on the interstate. I remember a young woman we encountered working in a tollbooth in Orlando. What made her unusual was that she didn't just take our money for the toll; she smiled and cheerfully told us to have a nice day, and was sincere. She was spreading sunshine and good energy on the interstate. She had a ripple effect.

We never know when someone needs that small, random act of kindness to change his or her day. I have heard stories of people on the verge of committing suicide who received a smile, recognition, or a glance from a stranger, a random act of kindness, and that caused them to change their mind.

Notice what ripples you are sending, and as always, feel good!

Summary and Suggestions

Everything is energy and all energy vibrates, including you and me. Energy equals vibration. We know we have different frequencies of energy, or vibration. This frequency depends on our own thoughts and feelings. The Law of Attraction doesn't decide if we deserve something or not; we decide through our thoughts and feelings. Abundance can be anything – relationships, money, job, health and happiness – really anything you want.

- Climb the ladder and reach for the feeling of relief. Enjoy that, and then reach for the next better feeling.
- Ask yourself the miracle question. What would your ideal life look like?
- Focus on what you want, not on what you don't want.
- If you can't have positive thoughts about something, don't think about it at all. Take it off your radar screen.
- Pay attention to what side of the twelve-inch ruler you are on most of the time.
- Develop and play abundance games; notice all the abundance around you.
- Notice what your dominant thoughts and feelings are. Do you see the glass half full?
- Balance your energy by swinging your arms across your body as you walk.
- Practice EFT to bring your intense emotions to neutral.
- Surround yourself with good energy and protect yourself from negative energy.
- Practice random acts of kindness to spread the ripple of good energy.

In the next chapter, we'll discuss how our thoughts and feelings affect our energy and lives.

Second Key – The Power of Our Thoughts and Emotions

"You are today where your thoughts have brought you; you will be tomorrow where your thoughts take you."
~ James Lane Allen, American author (1849-1925)

We often can't control the outside world. Life is what it is, and things happen. Our inside world, however, is made up of our thoughts and feelings, and that is more powerful than any outside force. We can control our inside world by paying attention to our thoughts and feelings, and choosing to allow good thoughts to govern our lives. No one can do that for us; we have the control. In fact, we can't make choices for anyone else, but the flip side is that no one can make choices for us, either.

Scientists estimate that the average person will think at a rate of between one and four thoughts per second while awake. Our minds process about 60,000 thoughts each day, and 95 percent of these thoughts are what we thought about yesterday. Eighty percent of the 60,000 habitual thoughts will be negative. This means that by the end of today, the average person will have had 45,000 Automatic Negative Thoughts (ANTs). Since our mind controls everything we do, it makes sense that our thoughts have tremendous impact on our actions and our lives. Creating a positive mindset is the first step in creating good health, happiness and abundance.

Researchers have measured blood flow and activity patterns in the brain while participants were having both positive and negative thoughts. They found that negative thoughts stimulate areas of the brain linked to depression and anxiety. They also learned that positive thoughts had a calming, beneficial effect on the brain. In other words, negative thoughts can be toxic to the brain, while positive thoughts and feelings are like good medicine. We all have more drugs in our brain than any drug company could ever make.

It's important to become more aware of your automatic thoughts, especially the negative ones. When you catch yourself thinking something negative such as, "Oh, that will never happen... I'm so fat... I'm never going to find the right partner...I'm not going to be able to do this," just acknowledge it, without judgment. Keep a tally for a day or so to show yourself just how many negative thoughts you have daily. Or notice what percentage of your waking day you have positive thoughts and what percentage you have negative thoughts. You may be surprised.

When you notice you are having negative thoughts, don't scold yourself, as that's negative, too. Simply acknowledge that thought and turn it into a positive one. It's another way to look at something. It's seeing challenges as opportunities and being thankful for what you do have at that moment. Our thoughts, and more importantly, our feelings influence how we perceive the world. We see what we expect to see.

Here are some examples of negative thoughts and a way to give them a positive spin:

Negative thought	Positive thought
I've never done this before.	This is an opportunity to learn something new.
It's too hard.	There is always more than one way to do something.
I can't do this myself.	I can accept help and maybe barter for this.
I'm too busy to do this.	How can I prioritize? What do I really need to do now?
This is just too much change.	I get to try something new, and I can say I did it.
No one is talking to me.	Gee, maybe they are just as shy as I am. I'll approach them instead.
I'll never find a relationship.	Maybe if I stop thinking about having a relationship, someone will find me.
I have so much pain.	I can still do things and so many people care about me.

We all have negative thoughts and that's normal, just don't let them control your life. Our feelings are even more critical. You can have a positive thought but still not feel good, because deep down at a subconscious level, you don't really believe it. You can always tell if the thought is truly positive or not by how you feel. The better you feel, the more positive your thoughts, the higher your vibration. Then you're on the right track.

Negative words and experiences stored in the subconscious mind end up affecting our emotions and feelings. Often we are not even aware of what is in our subconscious mind, yet that is what colors our world.

The Outer World

It's no wonder we see more anxiety and depression today than ever before. People start their day by drinking a cup of coffee and reading newspapers, magazines and websites that discuss accidents, earthquakes, suffering and poverty, among other negative issues. This does not help us start the day with positive thoughts or good feelings. Pay attention to what you read, watch, see, hear and discuss. Learn to be aware of your thoughts. This is especially important before you go to sleep. Negative issues will manifest in your life if you keep thinking about them. It's the mind chatter, the inner critic we all have telling us we are not good enough.

Our inner and outer worlds influence our health and our lives. Words we hear in our outer world affect us as well. Read these words slowly: depression, sadness, murder, rape, insult, cancer, assassination, betrayal, hell, torment, crying, bitterness, volcano, pain, suffering, earthquake, poverty.

What kinds of emotions do you feel now after reading those words? Do you feel some kind of pain in your body? Is your chest tight or are you slightly nauseated? Have these negative words affected your feelings and emotions?

Now, read these words: happiness, serenity, tranquility, appreciation, sincerity, gratitude, love, heaven, paradise, family, friends, God, dreams, hope, sunshine, compassion, kindness, nature, water, wealth, money, prosperity, loyalty.

What kinds of emotions are you experiencing now? What we hear or read in our outer world influences how we feel.

If you have had a stressful day or are worried about getting something done on time, you'll likely experience what I call "anxiety-laden dreams." These are the dreams where you can't get somewhere or can't get something done, or can't finish what you are doing. We all dream, however, not everyone can easily recall their dreams, especially if they don't pay attention to them as they are waking up. Write down a word or phrase to remind you later. Pay attention to your dreams. Are they happy and leave you with a good feeling, or do you have anxiety-laden dreams?

When we dream, we work through our emotions and stressors from the day. Sometimes we wake up feeling even more tired than when we went to bed. We may not have slept restfully, as our brain was working overtime to deal with everything from the day. The thoughts we have just before we drift off to sleep are important. They influence our dreams and how well we rest.

Our brain is like a computer in the sense that it needs downtime to defrag, scan and update, just as a computer does. What we listen to and what we think about at bedtime determines how well our brain will rest. Every emotion is just an emotion, not good or bad, just a feeling. If we have a negative emotion, acknowledge that feeling, whatever it is, and then let it go.

Laughter is Good for Us

As children, we start out happy. We naturally daydream about things that make us feel good; we have imaginary friends and all sorts of adventures in our minds. Children laugh more than three hundred times a day while adults laugh an average of fifteen times a day (and that's on a good day). I know few people who giggle like a child. When is the last time you had a good belly laugh? Children are so uninhibited; they say what they think. Generally, people think they're cute and don't punish them.

Laughter is healthy for us. Laughter reduces the level of stress hormones like cortisol. It also increases the feel-good hormones, like endorphins, and strengthens our immune system. It helps manage the physical effects of stress. Have you experienced the cleansing feeling you get after a good laugh? Laughter provides a physical and emotional release. A good belly laugh exercises the diaphragm, contracts the abs, and even relaxes shoulder muscles. It provides a good workout for the heart, as well. Distraction is a wonderful tool, and laughter takes the focus away from stressful situations and negative emotions. Laughter can even burn calories, about fifty calories in ten to fifteen minutes of a really good laugh.

Humor gives us a more light-hearted perspective and helps us see things in a different way. It can change potential challenges into opportunities, and can be fun and exciting.

Laughter connects us with others and is contagious. Have you ever found yourself laughing when you hear a child giggle? No one can resist that sound. I always catch myself starting to laugh. If you bring more laughter into your life, you can help others as well. By elevating the mood of those around you, you can reduce your stress level as well as theirs.

As we grow older, we attend school and have responsibilities added to our lives. Children often are told to "stop looking out the window" or "stop daydreaming and pay attention" in class. While I appreciate that children need to learn while in school, sometimes this stifles our natural tendency, even our ability to daydream as adults.

We Should All Daydream

When we are young, we often see our parents and other adults exhibiting behavior that encourages us to believe that working hard and struggling is the way to live. As adults, life is so busy we often don't daydream enough. Daydreaming or fantasizing is healthy and can be a great relaxation technique. When you are relaxed, it reduces stress and improves your quality of life. Studies show that relaxation can lower your blood pressure, reduce anxiety and boost your immune system.

Ideally, we should have a balance of work, play, spirituality, relationships and alone time. Many people equate daydreaming and playing with being lazy and not working hard enough. I think daydreaming is essential to productivity. We are more energized and creative when we have time to play. I hear so many people say they can't wait until vacation. Daydreaming takes us on that vacation anytime we want.

"Susie" was struggling and needed a vacation. We did some vacation imagery. Susie went into a relaxed state and began to imagine. I asked questions to help her feel as though she was on vacation. For example, I asked her to notice her surroundings, what time of day it was, what the temperature was like, etc. Afterwards, she said, "Wow, I took my last vacation all over again. That was great." She imagined doing all the things she had done on vacation. She felt the joy, smelled the ocean air, savored the food and enjoyed the sunsets. She was amazed that she had been imagining for only about ten minutes, because it felt like days to her.

Daydreaming and imagery let you feel that wonderful vacation anytime you want. In our minds, time has no meaning so we can feel like we are somewhere for days, when really, it's only minutes.

Our culture doesn't look at daydreaming and "non-doing" favorably, yet I believe it is essential for our well-being. We so seldom take time to be alone and enjoy daydreaming, doing nothing, or just being. It has been said that we have become human "doings" rather than human beings.

Take time this week to daydream, have a good belly laugh, or just do nothing for a while. It's good for your health, so give yourself permission!

Emotions themselves are, of course, not unhealthy. On the contrary, they are a normal response to life events. Failure to acknowledge and express our emotions, however, IS unhealthy and is an important factor in illness. As children, "if you can't say something nice, don't say anything at all" was a common refrain. Many adults don't express their emotions because of this limiting belief.

We may continue to stuff our emotions because of a limiting belief embedded in our subconscious mind years ago. We subconsciously build layer upon layer of inner defenses to protect us from unpleasant feelings. However, strong emotions find a way to emerge. If we don't deal with or express unpleasant emotions, they can manifest as pain or illness. Sometimes writing a letter you'll never send, journaling, hitting something with a soft Nerf bat, or punching a pillow helps you express and release negative feelings.

Stress is a Part of Life

Let's face it. Our lives are busy and stress is everywhere. We can't live without it. Our lives are full of hassles, deadlines, demands and frustrations. Stress is a natural function of the body, and not all stress is bad stress. Did you know that some types of stress actually are good for you?

Eustress refers to what many call good stress or healthy stress. Eustress can motivate people to be excited about something. Dr. Hans Selye, an endocrinologist, coined the term eustress in 1974. He studied and wrote about the impact of stress on the mind and body.

Long-term benefits of good stress include enhancing emotional balance and confidence, a sense of being wanted and a general feeling of happiness. Physical exercise is an excellent example of good stress. This type of stress prepares the muscles, heart and mind for the strength needed for whatever is about to occur. Engaging in physical activity, such as walking, running or working out in a gym, places stress on the body. It also releases endorphins that help elevate mood and protect individuals from depression.

Distress is a negative type of stress. There actually are two types of distress:
- Acute stress is the type of stress that occurs immediately when something changes and we have not yet adjusted to it. It messes up our normal routine. It is an intense type of stress, but it passes quickly.
- Chronic stress occurs if there is a constant change of routine. We are out of our norm, uncomfortable, overwhelmed and not feeling as though we are in control of our lives. Chronic stress affects the body for a long period of time. Someone who constantly moves or changes jobs experiences this type of stress. Almost everyone with a severe, life-threatening or

chronic illness can recall some significant, long-term stress about eighteen to twenty-four months before discovering their illness. It may have been a bad relationship or divorce, or a long period of time caring for someone else and not attending to his or her own needs.

Bad or destructive stress in small doses is not harmful. It sometimes helps us perform better under pressure. However, when we are constantly running in the fight-or-flight mode, our mind and physical body pay the price. Chronic stress can cause major health problems and weaken our immune system.

Life in general is stressful. Have you ever been stressed for a prolonged period of time and find it just zaps your energy and tires you out? Stress actually takes our energy away.

"Mike" developed multiple sclerosis. He said he had been in an unhappy marriage for many years prior to his diagnosis. I often find long-term stress and trauma are like planting seeds that grow into illness. The key is to get out of caustic situations. It takes a toll in many ways.

Almost everything – from playing sports, falling in love, getting ready for the holidays, to being on the frontline of war – involves stress. Therefore, to have stress is to experience life. Unfortunately, people who are quick to identify all stress as bad may lose the benefit of the good stress in their lives. The degree of stress we experience and the effect it has on our health partially depends on how we look at it.

Many people these days struggle with financial stress of one form or another. "Alice" found herself laid off from her job and she was very worried about finances. She had a well-paying job, so losing it really took a chunk out of her family's income. Even with unemployment, she knew it would be tough to make ends meet. She was feeling severely depressed, to the point of not wanting to go on. She didn't even want to wake up in the morning. She was not exactly happy in her previous job, but it paid the bills. She did some daydreaming and imagined what her perfect job would be like. She loved animals, especially dogs, and imagined herself managing a shelter for stray and unwanted puppies. She imagined how she would feel watching all the puppies run around and play in the yard. She imagined other people helping care for the puppies, and she could really see in her imagination how much they loved them, too. This made her feel good. She imagined how she would feel if this was her life and how thankful she would be if she could be this happy at a job and have financial security as well. After she daydreamed about her ideal job, she felt much better and was excited about the next day when she could update her resume and find a job where she could feel like this.

People who define and manage stress correctly, with a positive attitude and seeing the glass half full rather than half empty, enjoy greater amounts of eustress. As a result, they enjoy a full and enriching life. Stress is a necessary part of life. Its effect depends on you.

Two-Minute Relaxation Technique

A simple breathing technique can help tremendously in dealing with stressors in our lives, allowing us to take a moment to relax. There are many breathing techniques, but my favorite is a combination of several I have learned over the years. To watch a video of this technique, go to www.bonniegroessl.com.

To do this technique, sit with your ankles crossed (not your knees), arms out in front of you with the back of your hands turned inward and your palms facing outward. Cross one arm over the other (whichever way is comfortable for you; your body will automatically go the right way, so trust it). Interlock your fingers and rest your arms in your lap. Make sure you're comfortable. (Feel free to modify this technique. If it's not comfortable to sit this way, put your hands together in some way, cross something if you can, but just be comfortable.)

Next, gently place your tongue just behind your upper front teeth. You may be familiar with acupuncture points, which are located along meridian lines. Recall that meridians are the channels through which *chi* (energy) flows to nourish and energize the human body. Your tongue is behind your upper front teeth because you have two main meridians in the center of your body (governing and central meridian). One begins at the roof of your mouth, goes up and over your head and down your spine, links to the other meridian line, and comes all the way back up again. However, there is a little space right behind your upper front teeth where the meridians do not meet, so when you put your tongue there, it closes the circuit. All that energy you are moving is staying inside. This is a bilateral system, and by crossing your arms and ankles, you're crossing some of those meridian lines as well.

Rest your arms in your lap, and breathe in through your nose and out through your nose or mouth. When you breathe in, let the air fill your lungs without trying too hard or forcing it. When you breathe out, make that exhalation last as long as you can. Let all the air out, slowly, like a balloon slowly emptying. Notice the stillness at the end of the exhalation. Inhale again, breathing in easily and effortlessly. By breathing in through your nose and enjoying a nice, long exhalation, you're activating the relaxing side of you – your parasympathetic system. This calms you. Keep breathing in through the nose and out through the nose or mouth. Keep your tongue at the roof of your mouth, just behind your front teeth, if you can. Focus on your breathing and begin relaxing your muscles one by one. You may want to do this in front of the mirror. It will give you a mental picture of what you look like when you are in this position.

If you can't actually get into this position, say you're driving a car, you can use your imagination and it still will work. Our brain doesn't know the difference between real and imagined. I was having a painful physical therapy session once and I couldn't be in this position, so I just used my imagination. I tolerated the therapy well and I didn't feel the discomfort as much.

Thoughts Become Things

Few people realize what they actually are thinking about. Do you know what you think about? The life you lead reveals the answer. If you are happy and successful, you think thoughts of happiness and success. If you are struggling through life, feeling like you never have enough, thoughts of doubt, failure, fear, anger and helplessness are likely the cause. In other words, whether you think life is miserable or great, that's probably how it's playing out. Life is whatever we think it is.

Many thoughts are subconscious and we usually aren't even aware of them. Those little tapes playing in the background of our minds carry tremendous power. Consciously or not, before every spoken word, there is a thought. In the same way, there is a thought before every action. Since thoughts shape our words and behaviors, they inevitably shape our environment, relationships and future.

The biggest difference between people is their thoughts. Some people think learning is enjoyable and fun, while others dread learning. It's how we think about everything that majorly affects our lives. It colors our world and influences our reality. Sometimes people say our thoughts create our reality. In effect, what is actually happening is that we see and experience what we think about, consciously and subconsciously.

"Trudy" was told that eating cheddar cheese was a trigger for her migraine headaches. It was a food that migraine sufferers are told to avoid. While it's true that aged cheese can be a common trigger for migraines, everyone's body is different. For years, Trudy avoided cheddar cheese, but still had headaches, as there can be many things that trigger migraines. Even the aroma of cheddar cheese would cause a migraine. She really likes cheese, but for years didn't dare eat any because she was sure it was dangerous for her.

One day, she was at a workshop and the speaker was talking about triggers and how we become programmed to associate certain things with certain reactions. She decided to change her belief about cheddar cheese. She spent some time convincing herself that she could change this and she was in control of her headaches. After some work, she tested this belief by eating some cheddar cheese, all the while telling herself that she didn't have to have this association. She was able to not only smell, but also eat the cheese and she didn't get a headache. She kept it to moderation and was careful not to eat cheese when other triggers were present, like weather and hormone changes. Trudy learned that our thoughts can sometimes become things, even physical things.

What we eat, drink and breathe, and how we exercise feeds our physical body. Our thoughts and feelings from our inner world feed our minds. Our mind changes our brain, and that changes who we are.

Bruce Lipton, author of *The Biology of Belief,* is a scientist who began his career as a cellular biologist, studying stem cells. Lipton is now a leader in bridging the gap between science and spirit (www.brucelipton.com). He says that genes/DNA do not control our biology. Extra-cellular signals control our DNA. This includes the energetic messages coming from our positive and negative thoughts. Both the inner and outer world play huge roles, and how we perceive our environment can affect and alter gene expression.

We are made of trillions of cells. By retraining our mind to create healthy beliefs, we can change the physiology of our bodies. Epigenetics is a term used to describe situations in which genes express themselves differently, although the underlying DNA is the same. Dawson Church, PhD, has written many books on health, psychology and spirituality. He founded the Soul Medicine Institute, a nonprofit organization dedicated to research in this area. In *The Genie in Your Genes,* he talks about how our body reads our mind, and thus, gene expression changes (www.dawsonchurch.com).

Our Brain and the Subconscious Mind

The brain is basically two halves connected by a band of fibers called the corpus callosum. Think of that as the bridge between the two hemispheres of the brain. This helps messages get back and forth. For most people, the left brain is primarily responsible for speaking, writing and understanding language. It thinks logically and analytically, and identifies itself by the name of the person to whom it belongs – I am. The left brain is time bound and thinks in terms of past and future.

The right brain, in contrast, thinks in pictures, sounds, spatial relationships and feelings. The right brain is timeless; it only knows "now." The left brain analyzes, taking things apart, while the right brain synthesizes, putting pieces together. The left brain is a better logical thinker, while the right brain is more attuned to emotions. The left brain is most concerned with the outer world of culture, agreements, business and time, while the right brain is more concerned with the inner world of perception, physiology, form, emotion and intuition.

The left side of the brain is responsible for all logical external thinking: math, driving, using a computer or solving a puzzle. These activities require logical thinking and problem solving. We live our lives day by day without realizing what our brain is really doing.

The right brain has a special relationship with emotions and imagery. Many studies show that the right brain recognizes emotion in facial expressions, body language, speech and even music. This is critical because emotions are not only psychological, but also physical states. Although the subconscious mind seems to be more associated with the right hemisphere of the brain, it is much broader and not confined within the physical brain itself.

Communicating with the subconscious happens automatically, but not consciously. As we go through life, certain experiences shape certain beliefs into our minds without us even realizing it. These beliefs become conditioned responses. We don't even realize they are programs. For example, let's say a dog attacked you when you were young. This experience had such an effect on your subconscious mind that to this day, you are afraid of dogs. That fear/phobia is now a conditioned response. If you know how to effectively communicate with your subconscious, you can rewrite that response and remove that phobia completely.

We can't really see our mind; it doesn't show up on an MRI or CT scan. However, if you could see your mind, it would look like an iceberg. Picture an iceberg. That little bit we can see above the water is like our conscious mind. That's what we know we are thinking. The conscious mind is not very big and that is why shear willpower is not very powerful sometimes.

However, there's more iceberg underwater. That huge piece of the iceberg we can't see, that is like our subconscious mind. Some people call it the unconscious mind. Everything we've ever experienced is in our subconscious mind, all stacked up like a deck of cards. The good, the bad, the ugly ... all of it. We all have a metaphorical pile of dirt that we may have been adding to all our lives. We may have unpleasant life experiences, negative situations, berating comments and limiting beliefs we have accumulated throughout life. It behooves us to have the good stuff at the top of that pile; ideally, it's good to have some daisies growing at the top.

Current research shows that about 90 percent to 95 percent of what we say, do, think and feel every day is influenced by what's at the top of that stack in your subconscious mind. The good stuff is still there, it's probably just a little buried. What's at the top of your pile?

The conscious mind sets goals and thinks abstractly. It's in either the future or the past, and it's time bound. It has a limited processing capacity. Short-term memory is approximately twenty seconds, so if it takes you more than twenty seconds to walk into a room and you forgot what you were going to do, don't feel bad. If we're distracted, our short-term memory gets even shorter. Our conscious mind stores one to three events at a time and averages two thousand bits of information per second. That's a lot of information, but nothing compared to the subconscious mind.

The subconscious mind, which is most closely related to the right hemisphere of the brain, is more habitual, like autopilot. It monitors all the operations of the body, heart rate, digestion and breathing. It thinks literally, like a small child. It's what keeps everything working so we can walk, sit in a chair and go about our day. It thinks in present time only; the only time that exists is now.

The subconscious mind has expanded processing capabilities. Even though it thinks in present time only, it stores our long-term memory, past experiences, attitudes and beliefs. That's where we get into the science behind how everything that we have ever experienced is in our subconscious mind. It stores thousands of events at a time. It keeps us sitting up in a chair without falling down and keeps all our muscle fibers working together. It stores about 4 billion bits of information per second. That is billion with a "B." That is a lot of information per second. The vastness of our subconscious mind is indescribable. I often say the mind is like space, it's unlimited.

As humans, we tend to remember negative experiences much more than we remember the good things that happen in our lives. Have you ever had someone say something to you and you felt badly? That thought stayed with you for a long time. The rest of the day may have been perfectly fine – you may have had many positive experiences and interactions – yet that negative thought is the one that sticks with you. It becomes an automatic negative thought, an ANT.

We all have limiting beliefs as well as life-enhancing beliefs.

Limiting beliefs are things we may have heard or experienced in the past that negatively color the way we see the world. They get in our way, keeping us stuck or limiting us in some way. As an example, many of us grew up hearing that we have to "work hard for what we want." We wind up having a difficult time imagining that we can have anything without working hard to get it. We also may believe we are not worthy or deserving of what we want. Often, we are told as children that we must "work hard to get ahead," so as adults we feel like we are being lazy or feel guilty if we sit and enjoy just being.

Life-enhancing beliefs are formed by experiences that make us feel good, such as when people say or do things that help us feel confident and good about ourselves. It helps us feel as though we can do anything.

Limiting beliefs are formed by experiences that did not make us feel good. Perhaps we felt we failed at something, or were told we couldn't do it or didn't deserve it. As adults, many of us carry around more limiting beliefs than life-enhancing beliefs. These subconscious beliefs serve as filters to our reality. We all see reality in a different way because each of us has different beliefs. Three people can hear the same story or see the same event, yet they all may perceive it differently based on their subconscious beliefs and previous experiences.

I would bet most people have more limiting beliefs at the top of their subconscious stack than good, life-enhancing beliefs. We all know people who are positive and happy; we just feel good being around them. These people have more of the good stuff at the top. However, for most people, life gets in the way. What we are experiencing is often what we think about because it's in our face, especially if we are experiencing something unpleasant. It keeps our attention focused on that experience.

As humans, we tend to develop learned responses, certain habits and ways of thinking. Our brain actually changes to facilitate this, creating new pathways. Take physical pain as an example. Pain cannot be felt without the brain. Pain begins in nerve pathways from the brain to the body, and it becomes hard-wired over time into the circuitry of the brain. The central nervous system learns to create chronic pain even if there is no apparent medical condition causing the pain. A good example of this is phantom limb pain, where people feel pain in the area where an amputated limb used to be.

In the last twenty-five years or so, we have learned much more about the brain, and there is still a lot we don't know. The human brain is incredibly adaptive. Neuroplasticity is the brain's ability to reorganize itself by forming new nerve cell connections throughout life. I like to say this means the brain is plastic. We can mold it, like clay, and change it, like silly putty. This special characteristic allows the brain's estimated 100 billion nerve cells, also called neurons, to constantly create new pathways for neural communication and rearrange existing ones throughout life.

Without the ability to make such functional changes, our brains would not be able to memorize a new fact or master a new skill, form a new memory or adjust to a new environment. We would not be able to recover from a brain injury or overcome cognitive disabilities. Because of the brain's neuroplasticity, old dogs, so to speak, regularly learn new tricks. Neuroplasticity can work in two directions; it is responsible for deleting old connections as frequently as it enables the creation of new ones.

Sometimes when we have certain thoughts, feelings or experiences for an extended period of time, we create what I refer to as "grooves" in our brain and we get stuck. Take depression as an example. If a person is struggling with despair and sadness, fear or feeling overwhelmed for a long time, we create a rut or a groove, and it becomes the only way we know how to feel.

The good news is we can create new pathways around those feelings, and with practice, we can form a new groove, so to speak. When we engage our brain in new ways, we create new pathways for neural communication. Thus, neuroplasticity enables us to learn a new way of being.

It doesn't happen overnight, but it doesn't have to take years, either. In about thirty days, we can begin to create new pathways if we really work on it. That means most of the time we want to be focusing on the new way of being and how that feels. We can retrain our nervous system and brain to create a new response and get out of the painful rut that was created, whether it's physical or emotional pain.

Dr. Howard Schubiner has developed a program that helps people with pain issues unlearn the pathways that keep you in pain in his book, *Unlearn Your Pain*.

Hypnosis Happens - More Than We Realize

We have all been hypnotized many times in our life, and we don't even know it. There are really only two things required for hypnosis: a focused state of attention and a suggestion. We have all experienced this without referring to it as hypnosis. Have you ever been watching a movie or reading a good book, completely unaware of what was going on around you? If so, you were probably in a trance or hypnotic state. Perhaps you were driving on a familiar route and you suddenly couldn't remember if you stopped at the last stop sign. If so, you likely experienced what's known as "highway hypnosis."

Some practitioners teach self-hypnosis as a tool to enhance their patients' self-healing abilities. When we concentrate and focus, we're able to use our minds more powerfully. Mental imagery is powerful, especially when used in a focused state of attention. Our subconscious mind – that part of us that knows us best – has all the answers. But sometimes we are influenced by what others say or how they act, and we become hypnotized. Remember, we often get what we expect!

Think of how many times you or people you know have been sitting in a doctor's office or waiting for a test result. You're probably in a focused state of attention, that's the first part of hypnosis. Then the doctor or health-care provider arrives with the test result. Depending on what they say, and more importantly, what you hear, this becomes the suggestion. Boom, you have been hypnotized!

How many times have you been in a situation like that? It may not have been in a doctor's office, it may have been at work, school or home, but it happens more often than you think. Don't let others hypnotize you into believing what to expect in your life.

"Mary's" cancer had returned, and she was sitting in the exam room of her doctor's office, waiting for her test results. She was worried and was in a focused state of attention. The doctor came in, and I don't know exactly what he said, but she heard "you are going to die soon." I believe she was hypnotized into believing this. A few weeks later, she saw a different oncologist who told her that her type of cancer was chronic and similar to having diabetes. He said she may need treatment from time to time, but she could live a long time with this illness. She didn't hear a word he said; she didn't believe him. The nocebo effect had already hypnotized her into believing she would die soon.

People who are authority figures, like teachers, parents and health-care providers, are more likely to hypnotize us because of who we perceive them to be. They don't mean to do it; they don't even realize they are doing it.

When "Kathy" was in grade school, her music teacher told her not to sing with the rest of the class. He said she was probably tone deaf and she should just mouth the words at the concert. The music teacher embarrassed her in front of the class. Kathy is in her fifties now, and to this day, does not sing. I know there are voice teachers who would argue that anyone can sing, but Kathy was hypnotized to believe she could not.

We are prone to suggestions and hypnosis when we are in a state of focused attention. Because we see these people as authority figures, what they say or what we hear influences us. The way we perceive things in life is based on our past experiences as well as our thoughts, feelings and beliefs in our subconscious minds. The good news is we can undo those pre-hypnotic suggestions. We can learn techniques to change those limiting beliefs so they don't govern our lives.

In the clinical setting, we often use deep relaxation as a focused state of attention or trance state. While in this focused, relaxed state, we are able to access the power of our subconscious mind more effectively to make the changes we want and achieve the goals we desire. Recall that our subconscious mind is more powerful than we may think, influencing about 90 percent of what we do, say and think every day.

Clinical hypnosis is a method of communication that induces a trance or a trance-like state. It is an interaction in which a person responds to suggestions given by a hypnotherapist for imaginative experiences involving changes in perception and behavior. The hypnosis can be either authoritarian or permissive. Authoritarian hypnosis uses phrases such as "you will." The more permissive style uses phrases like "you may."

Ericksonian hypnosis is another method. Rather than giving specific suggestions, the hypnotherapist uses stories, metaphors and analogies about the topic, and allows the individual's subconscious mind to take the ideas from these stories and metaphors to create solutions. Our subconscious mind has all the answers anyway. Bill O'Hanlon, an inspirational speaker and prolific author who was trained as a psychotherapist, notes that Ericksonian hypnosis simply plants seeds of possibilities (www.billohanlon.com).

We all carry negative suggestions in our subconscious mind. Whether it's a previous hypnotic suggestion or a limiting belief based on something we heard as a child, the result is the same: it keeps us stuck, missing out on the life we want.

You or a hypnotherapist can undo any limiting belief or previous hypnotic suggestion that doesn't serve you well.

Can You Imagine?

In Dr. Martin Rossman's book, *Imagery for Self Healing,* he notes that imagery is a flow of thoughts we can see, hear, smell or taste. Imagery is our most fundamental language. The mind processes everything we do through images. When we recall events from our past or our childhood, we think of pictures, images, sounds, pain and so on. It's rarely through words. Images aren't necessarily limited to visuals, but also can be sounds, tastes, smells or a combination of sensations. A certain smell, for example, may invoke either good or bad memories.

Not everyone's primary way of perception is visual, so don't be concerned if you don't "see" images. When you use imagery, just accept whatever you experience. If you revisit a place where you had a bad experience, it may instantly bring memories of the situation. You may see images from that event or you may feel things, hear sounds or notice smells. You are really using your imagination, it's not really happening. It may initiate the body's fight-or-flight response, which is the body's response to a perceived threat or danger. During this reaction, the body releases certain hormones like adrenalin and cortisol, increasing the heart rate, slowing digestion, shunting blood flow to major muscle groups, and giving us a burst of energy and strength. Originally this physiological process was named "fight or flight" for its ability to enable us to physically fight or run away when faced with danger. Our sympathetic nervous system activates during the fight-or-flight response. This causes difficulty in thinking clearly and increases pain, as well as the symptoms already mentioned. These days, situations where our lives aren't in danger, like being stuck in traffic or having a stressful day at work, also can activate this response.

When people with Post Traumatic Stress Disorder (PTSD) have a flashback, they see the event as though they are experiencing it now – the sounds, feelings, smells – yet it's not really happening. The event seems so real that they may actually have physical changes, such as increased heart rate and blood pressure, perspiration or trouble breathing. Sometimes it can be a challenge to re-orient themselves to the here and now and know that they are safe, that they are not really experiencing the event. When the perceived threat or flashback is gone, systems usually return to normal. However, in times of chronic, everyday stress, this doesn't happen enough, which can damage the body. Some people stay in this fight-or-flight mode. Many people are sympathetic nervous system-dominant because of chronic stress, or physical or emotional pain.

We have the ability to escape the fight-or-flight response, return our system to normal, and provide time away from chronic stress. With imagery we can take a break, and in our mind, go somewhere pleasant and relaxing. Imagery can be instrumental for our well-being. It is also the window into our inner world and the subconscious mind.

Oftentimes people say they can't do imagery because they are not good at visualizing. I ask them if they have ever worried. I have never met a person who can honestly say they have never worried about something in their lives. Well, worrying is using your imagination. It's using it in a negative way, but it's using your imagination nonetheless. Most of the time, it's not what really is happening that causes us so much stress, it's what we imagine could happen that stresses us. The situation hasn't really happened; we are just imaging it.

The Power of Imagery

Try this simple exercise to use your imagery abilities. Slowly read this script to yourself or have someone read it to you:

"Relax for a moment and imagine you are holding a ripe, plump lemon. Feel its skin and notice its bright yellow color. Imagine putting it up to your nose and smelling it. Perhaps you can imagine what it smells like. Now imagine you are putting the lemon on a cutting board, taking a sharp knife and cutting off a slice. As you slice into the lemon, the juice squirts out and sprays onto the counter. Now imagine picking up the lemon wedge you have cut, smell it, and take a big bite into it, allowing the sour juices to squeeze into your mouth. Did you salivate or pucker as you imagined cutting and tasting the juicy lemon?"

Imagery can be helpful in motivating change or creating a feeling that you are already where you want to be. It also can alert you to possible limiting beliefs or barriers that may prevent you from attaining long-term success.

It's not uncommon for people to have some anxiety when they think about losing weight, for example, especially if they have been overweight for a long time, or have gained and lost and gained weight again. Using imagery helps you actualize your goals and alerts you to any potential barriers. Anything is possible in your imagination. It's a great way to feel as though you've already achieved your goal and can imagine what that feels like. Choose a successful ending, such as meeting a goal. Pretend you have already achieved this goal; it's not something in the future.

Choose just one goal for the purpose of this exercise:
"Imagine you can see yourself having accomplished your goal, see yourself in the mirror. What do you see? It may be easiest to look at yourself as though you are far away, and then gradually bring your image closer into view.

"Notice what time of day it is as you are looking in the mirror. What does your face look like? What does your body look like, now that you've achieved your goal? Do you have a different posture? Imagine hearing two people important to you acknowledging that you have reached your goal, congratulating you on your success. Hear how you respond. How did you announce to these people that you reached your goal? What did your friends say in response? Can you hear the tone of their voice? Take in the affirmation and congratulatory remarks, and feel good."

Mental imagery is a powerful tool, especially in a focused state of attention. Imagery may be actually visualizing or "seeing," but it may also be feeling, hearing, smelling or using any of the senses. In a state of concentrated attention, ideas and suggestions that are compatible with what you want have a powerful impact on the mind, especially the subconscious mind.

When you are listening to suggestions and imagery, it is best if you are in the same position each time as, eventually, simply being in this position will promote relaxation and a focused state of attention. As you use these techniques, take what fits for you and leave the rest. Feel free to change the words if you make your own recording of the relaxation script. We are all individuals, and different people will identify more with certain suggestions. For best results, I suggest you practice imagery or listen to a recorded script more often in the beginning. If you listen to a recording, you may find that after a while, you may not need to listen to it on a regular basis and will use it only as you feel the need.

Here are some additional imagery and relaxation scripts. Either record yourself reading these slowly, or have someone read them to you or record them for you. You also can write your own script and record it.

Guided meditation audios also are available on my website (www.bonniegroessl.com). **Please do not listen to these recordings while you're driving!**

Induce a State of Deep Relaxation for Hypnosis

"To begin, get in a comfortable position, close your eyes, and focus your attention on your breathing. Whenever you are ready, you can take a deep breath through the nose, and exhale this first breath out of your mouth. Then, continuing to breathe in and out through your nose, feel the air coming in through your nose and going down to your abdomen ... as you slowly exhale, let your abdomen relax and deflate letting all tension go with your exhale. Feel the tension flowing from your body with each exhalation.

"As you continue breathing, you may notice that you relax more and more with every breath. You may notice the muscles in your scalp and face begin to relax with every breath; your eyes become heavier, your jaw relaxes, your neck muscles loosen. It feels like a warm, comfortable, progressive wave of relaxation spreading down your body, leaving you more and more relaxed with every breath. Down to your shoulders, comfortable warmth spreading, a feeling of total relaxation ... loose, limp muscles spread down your arms to your elbows

... *all the way down to your wrists and hands ... allowing any remaining tension to flow out of your fingertips. You may notice that you feel somewhat more relaxed than you did when you started ... you may even notice that as you continue to breathe, you feel more and more relaxed.*

"As you continue to breathe, your chest and upper back begin to loosen, relax ... loose, limp muscles ... down to your abdomen and lower back ... loosening, relaxing, becoming more and more relaxed with every breath. Loose, limp muscles, feeling comfortably heavy and warm ... down to your hips and thighs ... spreading down to your knees, ankles and feet ... allowing any remaining tension to flow out your toes. Know that as you continue to breath, you will become even more relaxed with every breath."

Imagery Exercise: Evoke a Feeling

First, think about what feeling you would like to evoke or experience. Maybe it's a feeling of being relaxed or that of feeling energized. Perhaps it's a feeling of confidence – you may be anxious about performing well at something, like a test or sport. If you have pain issues, you may want to feel comfortable and move effortlessly. However you would like to feel, you can! And you can bring that feeling into the future whenever you need it.

Follow this script.

"To begin, get in a comfortable position, close your eyes, and focus your attention on your breathing. (Pause) Whenever you are ready, take a deep breath in through the nose, and exhale this first breath out of your mouth. This is giving your body a signal that it's time to go inside and use your imagination. Then, continuing to breathe in and out comfortably through your nose, at your own pace, feel the air coming in through your nose and going down to your abdomen ... as you slowly exhale, let your abdomen relax and deflate, letting go of all tension ... with the out-breath. Feel the tension flowing from your body with every exhalation.

"As you continue breathing, you may notice that you relax more and more with every breath. You may notice the muscles in your scalp and face begin to relax; your eyes become heavier, jaw relaxing, neck muscles loosening, like a warm, comfortable, progressive wave of relaxation spreading down your body, leaving you more and more relaxed with every breath. Down to your shoulders, a comfortable warm feeling of total relaxation ... loose, limp muscles down your arms, to your elbows ... all the way down to your wrists and hands ...

allowing any remaining tension to flow out your fingertips. You may notice that you feel somewhat more relaxed than you did when you started ... you may even notice that as you continue to breathe, you will feel more and more relaxed ...

"As you continue to breathe ... your chest and upper back begin to loosen, relax ... down to your abdomen and lower back ... loosening, relaxing, becoming more and more relaxed with every breath. Loose, limp muscles, feeling comfortably heavy and warm ... down to your hips and thighs ... spreading down to your knees, lower legs and ankles and, finally, your feet ... allowing any remaining tension to flow out your toes. If there is any remaining tension, know that you can just breathe into that place and allow it to leave with the exhale. Knowing that, you may become even more relaxed with every successive breath.

"Now, knowing that you are relaxed and able to go into your imagination, I want you to go to a time where you felt just like how you would like to feel right now. It may be recent or it may be a long time ago, perhaps even when you were a child. Usually the first thing that comes to your mind is right. Or, you can simply just imagine what it will be like to feel this way. (Pause)

"Take a moment and notice where you are ... what do you notice in your surroundings? ... You may be outdoors or indoors ... you may be in nature, the comfort of your own home, or some other place. Are you there by yourself or are other people there? ... Notice what you hear ... what scents or smells are in the air? Is there a breeze or is it still? ... What time of day is it? ... What season? ... What is the temperature today? Look at yourself. What are you wearing? If you are barefoot, notice what the earth feels like beneath your feet. ... It feels so good to be here. You feel exactly how you want to in this place.

"Just enjoy this experience; it feels so good to be here and feel this way. You feel like you can do anything. Just enjoy this time being comfortable and relaxed ... it feels so good! (Pause)

"Is there a word that describes this feeling? ... Notice where you feel this feeling most in your physical body ... Is there a place? Sometimes people feel it most in their chest or belly, or perhaps you just feel it throughout your body in general ... notice where you feel it the most. If this feeling had a color, what color would it be? If this feeling could look like something, what would it look like? What shape would it have? ... How about a temperature? Does it seem warm, cool, any particular degree? ... If you could reach out and touch this feeling, this really good feeling ... what kind of texture would it have?

"If you would like, you can intensify this good feeling, just like turning up the volume on a CD player or radio. You can make it bigger, and bigger, and

bigger ... allowing it to fill every blood vessel, every nerve, every muscle of your body ... getting bigger and bigger ... filling every single cell of your body ... Let it reach to the very edges of your skin ... you can even let it go beyond the edges of your skin, like a blanket enveloping you in this feeling. (Pause)

"And when you have your feeling to just the right amount, the amount that's perfect for you ... you may want to give it a symbol, something to remind you of this feeling (some people imagine squeezing their thumb and forefinger together; some people think of a word, an image, or a sound to remind them of how good they feel right now). ... Know that just by relaxing a bit and using your symbol you can return to this feeling, anytime you want to, anytime you need to. This feeling is always there for you, and your symbol will bring it to the forefront whenever you need it ... whenever you want it. (Pause)

"Knowing that you can evoke this feeling anytime, you continue to feel good as you slowly come back to the awareness of your surroundings, the here and now. You begin to notice your breathing, bringing your attention back to the here and now. Keep this feeling as you slowly turn your attention back to the room, feeling the surface beneath you, feeling refreshed, healthy, and energized. ... Take all the time you need.

"You may want to take a deep breath or stretch, taking all the time you need to come back ... opening your eyes to a soft gaze whenever you are ready."

Imagery Exercise: The Secret Garden

"To begin, get in a comfortable position, close your eyes, and focus your attention on your breathing. Feel the air coming in through your nose and going down to your abdomen. As you slowly exhale, let your abdomen relax and deflate. Feel the tension flowing from your body with each exhalation. Continue breathing comfortably (a few more breaths) and then take a deep, full breath and exhale; take another full, even deeper breath and exhale slowly.

"Now I am going to take you to a very special place. Imagine lying on your back in a open meadow, looking at the clouds in the sky ... notice the color of the sky today and what the clouds look like, notice the temperature and what time of day it is ... a cloud gently reaches down and picks you up, softly, gently, holding you safe as it brings you across the sky to a very special place. You are floating across the sky in a huge, white, fluffy cloud. You are very relaxed and comfortable. There is no tension or stress in your body; all discomforts have disappeared.

"Your cloud sets you down at the gate to a beautiful garden. The gate is laced with beautiful flowers and magically opens in front of you. As you slowly walk into the garden, you see flowers of every color and fragrance. Butterflies fill the air and there are birds singing. A butterfly may light on you, just to say hello and welcome you. You walk among the flowers on a path of lush, soft, green grass that feels wonderful beneath your bare feet. Take some time to bend down and smell some of the flowers. Take some time to enjoy all the beauty, touch the flowers, smell the fragrances, and feel the soft, cushy grass beneath your toes. (Pause)

"As you look ahead on the path, there is a beautiful, inviting bench beckoning you to take a seat. You decide to take a rest. As you are sitting there, someone (it could be a person, an animal, a bird, any type of image) joins you, sits with you for a while. . . . This is one of your angels. You and your angel sit on the bench for a while, not saying a word. Your angel knows your burden, and tells you with her eyes that you should give your burden to her. Whether it is pain or discomfort, sorrow or worry, guilt or fear ... any burden you have. You know you can hand it to your angel and she will carry it for you.

"And so you sit with your angel while the weight is lifted from you, and it feels so wonderful ... to have peace. Enjoy this time. Take in the beauty of the garden in this peaceful state. Breathe in the peaceful serenity. (Pause)

"Now you realize it is time for you to leave. You thank your angel for the peace she has given you, and slowly rise to leave the garden. ... You may want to stop and smell the flowers one more time and say goodbye to the butterflies as they walk you to the gate, fluttering around you. Now you are at the gate, and you walk through, totally refreshed and at peace. ... Your cloud is waiting. It gently picks you up, keeping you safe and warm as it takes you back. You are still floating in the air, on your magic cloud, feeling so good ... so peaceful. Your cloud sets you down in this room. You slowly feel the chair (bed, or floor, etc.) beneath you, supporting you. . . . You begin to notice and feel your fingers and toes. You may notice sounds in the room around you. ... When you are ready to come back, slowly open your eyes to a soft gaze. Stretch if you feel like it, as you become fully aware of your surroundings."

Imagery Exercise: Take a Mini Mental Vacation

"To begin, get in a comfortable position, close your eyes, and focus your attention on your breathing. Whenever you are ready, you can take a deep breath through the nose, and exhale this first breath out of your mouth, giving your body a signal that it's time to go inside and take a little break. Then, *continuing to breathe in and out through the nose, feel the air coming in through your nose and going down to your abdomen ... as you slowly exhale, let your abdomen relax and deflate, letting all tension go ... with the exhale. Feel the tension flowing from your body with every exhalation.*

"As you continue breathing, you may notice that you feel more and more relaxed with every breath. You may notice the muscles in your scalp and face begin to relax, your eyes become heavier, your jaw relaxes, your neck muscles loosen. ... Like a warm comfortable progressive wave of relaxation spreading down your body, leaving you more and more relaxed with every breath; like being in a wonderful, warm shower. From your neck down to your shoulders, a comfortable, warm, spreading feeling of total relaxation ... loose, limp muscles ... down your arms, to your elbows ... all the way down to your wrists and hands ... allowing any remaining tension to flow out your fingertips.

"You may notice that you feel somewhat more relaxed than you did when you started ... you may even notice that as you continue to breathe, you will feel more and more relaxed ....

"As you continue to breathe ... your chest and upper back begin to loosen, relax ... loose, limp muscles ... down to your abdomen and lower back ... loosening, relaxing, becoming more and more relaxed with every breath. Loose, limp muscles, feeling comfortably heavy and warm ... down to your hips and thighs ... spreading down to your knees, lower legs, ankles and, finally, your feet ... allowing any remaining tension to flow out your toes. You will become even more and more relaxed with every breath as you continue to breathe.

"Now, knowing that you are relaxed and able to go into your imagination, I would like you to go somewhere, anywhere you would like to be, for a wonderful private vacation ... somewhere you can relax and enjoy. Perhaps it's a place you've been before, or maybe it's a place you are just imagining now. There are no limits; anything is possible in your imagination. ... Perhaps you are reliving a previous vacation, or just going to the beach, the mountains, or wherever you would like to go to feel really good. (Pause)

"Notice where you are and what's in your surroundings ... notice the colors and textures ... there may be trees, a beach, mountains, buildings ...

"Are you there by yourself or are there other people? ... Notice what you hear ... Are there birds or animals ... What scents or smells are in the air? ... Is there is a breeze or is it still? ... If there is a breeze, can you feel it on your face or skin? What time of day is it in your private vacation? What season is it? ... What's the temperature? Is it warm or is it cool? ... Look at yourself and notice what you are wearing. If you are barefoot, notice what the earth feels

like beneath your feet. If you are on the beach, for example, the sand may be hot and dry, or cool and smooth if the tide just went out.

"What would you like to do on your vacation? You may want to just sit and relax, sipping a cool drink, or perhaps go for a leisurely walk along the beach or on a path in the forest. Maybe you just want to do some sight-seeing. Enjoy this experience ... there is nothing to do, no clock to watch, no worries, no phone, no interruptions ... just a carefree, calm feeling that allows you to relax and enjoy this time. (Pause)

"Enjoy the sights, sounds, smells, and tastes of this vacation. Anything is possible in your imagination, so if you have pain or problems moving, these issues do not keep you from doing anything you want to on your vacation. You can eat anything you want, be with anyone you want, or just be alone. There are no limits. There is no time reality here; it may seem like you are enjoying this vacation for a long time. Several days may go by in your mind.

"Just enjoy ... feeling comfortable, carefree, relaxed ... it feels so good! You now know that you can take a vacation anytime you want to, anytime you need to ... it's always available to you. You realize how good it feels to be this relaxed, and plan to take many mental vacations to help you ease stress and feel good!

"Knowing that you can take a vacation anytime you want to, slowly allow the images of your vacation to fade, but retain this relaxed, refreshed, renewed feeling as you slowly come back to the here and now. Continue to relax as you slowly come back to the awareness of your surroundings. You begin to notice your breathing, bringing your attention back to the here and now, knowing that you feel refreshed, healthy, and energized.

"You may want to take a deep breath or stretch as you take all the time you need to come back ... opening your eyes to a soft gaze whenever you are ready."

Self-Hypnosis: Weight Loss

"To begin, get in a comfortable position, close your eyes, and focus your attention on your breathing. Whenever you are ready, you can take a deep breath through the nose, and exhale this first breath out of your mouth. Then continuing to breathe in and out through the nose, feel the air coming in through your nose and going down to your abdomen ... as you slowly exhale, let your abdomen relax and deflate, letting all tension go ... with the exhale. Feel the tension flowing from your body with each exhalation.

"As you continue breathing, you may notice that you relax more and more with every breath. You may notice the muscles in your scalp and face begin to relax, with every breath; your eyes become heavier, jaw relaxing, neck muscles loosening ... like a warm comfortable progressive wave of relaxation spreading down your body, leaving you more and more relaxed with every breath ... Down to your shoulders, a comfortable warm, spreading feeling of total relaxation ... loose, limp muscles spreading down your arms, to your elbows ... all the way down to your wrists and hands ... allowing any remaining tension to flow out your fingertips. You may notice that you feel somewhat more relaxed than you did when you started ... you may even notice that as you continue to breathe, you will feel more and more relaxed ...

"As you continue to breathe ... your chest and upper back begin to loosen, relax ... loose, limp muscles ... down to your abdomen and lower back ... loosening, relaxing, becoming more and more relaxed with every breath. Loose, limp muscles, feeling comfortably heavy and warm ... down to your hips and thighs ... spreading down to your knees, ankles and feet ... allowing any remaining tension to flow out your toes ... knowing that as you continue to breath, you will become even more relaxed with every breath.

"Because you are now relaxed, you can be successful in reaching any goal ... at losing weight and becoming healthier. You imagine yourself looking thinner and toned; you look and feel great. You may want to imagine seeing yourself in the distance at first and then coming closer and closer to your new healthy, slimmer body. Your body is slimmer and toned, you feel strong and healthy. ... (pause) ... Your subconscious will now act on this image and make it happen. You allow yourself to let go of the weight, to let go of the weight, to let go of the amount of weight you no longer want or need, and you maintain the new slimmer, healthier body.

"You change negative eating patterns into good patterns now. You allow this to take place easily and effortlessly. And you imagine for a moment that you are in a room and there is a table in front of you. This table is filled with foods that are harmful to you, foods that are harmful to your body and emotions. You imagine these foods ... they are snack foods, candy, junk foods, cookies, and pastries.

"These foods are all harmful to you. They are like poison in your system. These kinds of foods cause you to gain weight and to feel sick. If you choose to eat any of these foods, you eat a very, very small amount ... even the smallest bite of these foods satisfies you completely and you will not gain weight and you will not feel sick, because this very, very small amount is enough to completely

satisfy you. ... You push these foods off the table, push them away from you. Your body and emotions reject these foods.

"Now, on the empty table, you place the many foods that you enjoy ... foods that are healthy, foods that contain good nutrition and fewer calories, foods that make you feel good when you eat them. It feels so good to have a healthy body. ... There are vegetables, luscious salads with dark greens, salads so delicious you hardly need any salad dressing, if at all, and colorful fruits. They are crisp and fresh and delicious just by themselves. You eat whole grains and lean protein, smell the fresh fruit, and you imagine you are in paradise, eating like royalty. ... You imagine eating these good foods, slowly, enjoying these healthy foods and your body feels great... it feels so good to feed your body foods that make you feel healthy and energized. Imagine eating, enjoying, savoring these foods, these good foods.

"Whether you are at a social event, at a buffet, at home, watching TV, talking, or eating in quiet ... you are eating very, very slowly ... you notice every bite you are putting in your mouth ... you savor the taste of these healthy foods. You are very aware of the amount of food you are eating, and you eat only a modest amount and then stop. ... and that feels perfect, just perfect. You eat correct and reasonable amounts and feel totally satisfied. You are totally satisfied. You are satisfied from one meal to the next, and when you do have a snack, it is a modest amount and a healthy food, because healthy foods make you feel so good. They are so delicious and you enjoy them.

"You find that moving, walking, and other exercise is appealing to you now and you enjoy moving your body and feeling physically fit. It feels so good to move; it feels so good to feel healthy, toned, and fit, to use your muscles, and to build up endurance, to feel healthy and strong. This makes you feel great and very proud of yourself.

"You are very proud of yourself. You reflect on all the positive things in your life ... and the goals and success you have already achieved, and you know you'll continue to be successful, reaching every goal you have, and creating the most healthy and positive life for yourself.

"And now imagine seeing yourself after reaching your goals. You look great and feel fantastic ... You look slimmer, toned, and physically fit ... you feel energized and proud of yourself for reaching your goals. You are relaxed and peaceful and food is less important to you now. You are comfortable eating slowly ... snacking is less important to you, is less important to you ... regardless of where you are or what you are working on -- at home, at work, or at social events. You can eat small amounts of food at a restaurant and you eat more

slowly, feeling completely satisfied, savoring your delicious, healthy foods. You may even leave some of your meal on your plate and that's fine, it's just fine.

"Regardless of your stress, you are more relaxed and at peace, and food is less important to you. You feel proud of yourself. The rewards are tremendous. Now, whenever you think of eating, you choose those good, healthy foods, and you eat the correct amount, and you feel completely satisfied, completely satisfied ... You stop eating at the correct amount and feel very good. You may even leave some food on your plate and that's OK. That's OK. You simply stop eating, and continue to relax.

"Allow that new sense of confidence and peace to flow through you. You are more motivated than ever before to create the healthiest eating patterns, to lose the weight you no longer want or need. You are more motivated to change your old eating patterns into goods eating patterns, and to maintain weight loss.

"You now have new ways to deal with your old habits. When you are at a social event, potluck, or buffet, you take only a small amount. You choose healthy foods, and you eat slowly, enjoying and savoring these healthy foods.

"When you get up in the morning, you find that moving, walking, and other exercise is appealing to you and you enjoy moving your body and feeling physically fit. You plan time during the day to take care of your physical body by moving, walking, and doing exercise you enjoy. It feels so good to move, it feels so good to feel healthy, toned, and fit. This makes you feel great and proud of yourself.

"These habits make permanent weight loss possible. You feel wonderful and you can begin to experience a new and healthy vital energy that flows through your body and mind. Your thoughts are positive, confident. You reflect on all the positive aspects about yourself, your intelligence, creativity. You are wonderful in so many ways. You see yourself as the attractive person that you are. And you allow these positive feelings to grow stronger and stronger for you every day, every day, every day.

"And now you continue to relax as you slowly come back to awareness of your surroundings. You begin to notice your breathing, bringing your attention back to the here and now. Knowing that you are successful in losing weight, the weight you no longer want or need ... feeling relaxed about food, taking care of your body and enjoying exercising and moving your body, feeling healthy and energized, feeling excited about making positive changes in your life, knowing you are successful.

"Imagine how your body physically feels, how you carry yourself now that you reached your goal. How do you feel and fit in your clothes? Do you sense *how you sit differently when in a restaurant? Do you feel lighter or have more energy?*

"Notice how you feel emotionally now that you've reached your goal. Feel the pride in your accomplishment, feel the confidence, the satisfaction ... enjoy these feelings. What aromas do you sense with your success? Smell them now. How does food smell now that you have reached your goal? How has your sense of smell changed now that you are successful?

"What tastes do you notice as you have reached your goal? Taste them now, Access whatever new tastes you can associate with your success. What does your favorite food taste like now that you are happy and at your goal?

"Enjoy the feeling of success ... come back to the room when you are ready. You may want to take a deep breath or stretch as you take all the time you need to come back ... opening your eyes to a soft gaze whenever you are ready."

Symptom Imagery

The feelings and physical symptoms we experience are usually trying to tell us something. It's like the oil light going on in the car. Illness is real, and accidents happen. Sometimes medicine is necessary. It is helpful to be in tune with our body and learn what our symptoms are trying to tell us. Imagery is a useful tool to communicate with our symptoms and learn the message.

"Carla" had Irritable Bowel Syndrome (IBS). She was afraid to go anywhere, fearing she wouldn't find the bathroom in enough time and would have an accident. IBS truly affected her life. She was afraid to go on trips, even go out to lunch with friends, because she didn't know what foods or situation might set off her condition. She was not working, and was afraid to return to work, even though her kids now were in school. She worked on some symptom imagery and learned what her body was trying to tell her.

Through practicing her imagery and meeting the image of her symptoms (an anxious, pacing cat), Carla discovered that anxiety was setting off the diarrhea and IBS symptoms. After working on this for a while, the anxious cat became a house kitten that needed attention and love. She found that, in her imagination, she was able to pet the kitten on her lap and soothe it. She subdued her symptoms and took control of her life again. She went on trips, out to lunch with friends, and even returned to work. She got her life back by dedicating time to practicing imagery and talking to her symptoms.

Imagery Exercise: Symptom Imagery

Here is a script to help you get in touch with your inner healer and explore what your symptoms might be trying to tell you. You can simply read it slowly, taking your time and really feeling like you are somewhere else, or read it and record yourself, or have someone read it or record it for you.

"First of all, get in a relaxed, comfortable place. It may be in a favorite chair or the comfort of your bed, and just begin to focus on your breathing. As you breathe in, feel all the life force coming in, and as you exhale, let go of anything you no longer need. The goal is to be relaxed and in that inner place that all of us have. So, as you continue to breathe, notice yourself feeling more relaxed. Imagine a white ball of healing energy in the center of your abdomen, and as you inhale, the ball moves up over your head and, as you exhale, it moves down your spine and into the ground. So, as you inhale, this ball of healing energy goes up and over your head. And, as you exhale, it goes down your spine and into the ground, taking with it all of the things you don't need right now. If that works for you, just imagine rolling that ball of healing energy around and around with every inhalation and every exhalation until you feel comfortable enough, and relaxed enough to go somewhere in your imagination.

"When you are to the point where you feel relaxed enough to go somewhere in your imagination, imagine where you would go. It may be the beach or a wooded area; it might be the comfort of your own bed. It doesn't really matter where you go, just so that you are relaxed. Once you are to that place, a place where you feel really good, rest there a bit. … Notice what time of day you think it is; notice the temperature in your surroundings. Is it warm, cool, a certain degree? Notice everything you can about being in that place where you feel really good and just hang out there for a while. … Just enjoy the peace of feeling good. … Notice what you are wearing, what you look like when you are in this place where you feel good.

"Are you standing, sitting, or are you lying down? Find a place, if you would like, where you really feel comfortable and take a rest for a while. … Just enjoy being there. … Notice where you are and how it feels. When you're relaxed and comfortable, just enjoy just being in that place where you feel good. … After a while, allow an image to form for that symptom that you are dealing with, whatever that symptom is. If it could look like something, what do you think it would look like? The first thing that pops into your mind is usually the right thing. … Take the image that comes to you, whatever that might be. It

might be an inanimate object, it might be a person or an animal, it might be a rock, or it might be just a shape or a color. Perhaps it's more of a feeling, a smell, or sound rather than an image. Take whatever comes.

"Just accept that image and notice everything there is to notice about it. Whether you sense it, smell it, feel it, see it, what do you notice? What is it like? Does your image seem hard, abrasive, soft, happy, not so happy? Simply notice everything that you can notice about it. ... If you are comfortable touching it, you can. See what texture it has. How big is it in relationship to you? How do you feel around it? ... How close is it to you? If you are uncomfortable and it's too close to you, you can ask it to move away a bit. See what happens. If nothing changes, maybe ask it what you need to do first for it to back off and be further from you.

"If there is anything you would like to find out from the symptom, go ahead and ask it. You may want to ask why it's here. What message does it have? Ask whatever you would like and then allow it to respond to you in any way you can understand. It might not be in words; it might be a feeling that you get. Know that you can engage in conversation with your symptom. Just let it respond in any way that you can understand and notice if it's changing in any way. If you don't want the symptom there, let it know that and see how it responds.

"Come from a loving place and perhaps ask it to go away. Or, ask what you need to do first so it can leave you alone. You could ask what one little thing you need to do so the symptom, the image, goes away or gets better, becomes smaller, or lessens. You may even want to ask the image if it has a name. Again, take whatever comes to you first. You could always ask, 'Would you be willing to meet with me again to continue this dialog?' Most of the time, it will be willing to meet with you again.

"It's always nice to thank your symptom for showing up and talking with you, and then, after you've said your thank you and goodbye, allow yourself to come back to the present time."

You will be amazed at what happens when you have a conversation with your symptoms. Establishing a relationship with symptoms is a powerful tool, and learning what they are trying to tell you can be helpful. You also can barter with your symptoms. Ask what you need to do for the symptom to lessen, and then set up a bartering agreement with it.

You don't have to have just one conversation. This can be ongoing daily dialog if you would like. You can set a time to meet. Let's say you want to meet with your symptom every morning. I suggest you keep those dates because it's like making a lunch date with a good friend. If you don't show up, they get a little irritated. So keep your dates and meet with your symptom.

Interactive Guided Imagery$^{(sm)}$ involves more than simply listening to a guided imagery script. It is interactive, just as the name implies. It's a powerful tool that can help you interact with your inner self, learn what your symptoms are trying to tell you, and make changes in your life. When we learn to interact with our inner selves, we can learn to manage our outward symptoms while often learning what we need to change to feel better. We have all the answers, and interactive guided imagery is a wonderful way to access that information. A practitioner may guide you through the imagery process as you learn how to interact with your inner self. You then can engage in regular conversations on your own to promote well-being. Sometimes our symptoms just need some attention and love – like a child who may act out for the same reason.

"Karen" was having a terrible time with abdominal pain. All of her testing was normal, and no one could explain the reason for her pain. She worked on some imagery about this. The image that represented her pain was a large knot, like the ones you see on ships. Through imagery, she asked what she could do to make the pain leave her alone. The answer that came was that she should have fun. She didn't focus on getting rid of the pain, but simply asked what she could do to help it go away.

The pain did subside and didn't bother her for a long time. Then, one day, when she was out having fun rollerblading with her husband, the abdominal pain reappeared. She knew that she had made a deal with the image of her pain, so she talked to her "knot." She told the knot she was doing what it asked her to do. She was having fun with her husband and she was keeping her end of the bargain, and "the knot" should keep its end, too. Her abdominal pain instantly went away. She felt better and was able to continue rollerblading with her husband and having fun. Karen felt empowered that imagery could help her physical situation. She felt like she had some control in her life.

Affirmations Can Be Powerful

Saying an affirmation is like talking to yourself. If you practice affirmations enough and believe what you are saying, you will begin to believe the statements. It becomes a life-enhancing belief. Affirmations can be a way to get what you want to the top of that stack in your subconscious mind, and shape your life the way you want. These types of statements are best if you are focusing on what you want and pretending you are already there.

When you are talking to the subconscious mind, remember that it's similar to talking with a small child. Little kids, three to five years old, don't understand the future; everything is here and now. Tell a child "tomorrow we are going to the zoo," and you will probably regret it because every five minutes they will ask, "Are we going? Is it zoo time? Is it tomorrow? Are we there yet?" Little kids don't understand the future. I think that's why they always ask, "Are we there yet?" when you take them somewhere in the car.

The other thing little kids don't understand until we teach them is the word "no." If we say, "don't do that," what they hear is, "do that." The "don't" doesn't exist. That's just like our subconscious minds. We need to keep this in mind when we are going to use an affirmation or talk to ourselves. You want to focus on what you want, but you also want to be in present tense and avoid any negative words. Beginning your statement with "I feel," "I am," "I have," "I know," or "I believe" is much more effective than using the future tense "I will." Future tenses could be fifty years from now, and you don't want to wait that long. The subconscious mind doesn't understand the future.

Affirmations, in and of themselves, are simply words. It's the feeling that you put into those words that makes the difference. You must believe what you are saying in an affirmation; that's what makes it powerful. If you are saying the affirmation aloud, say it as though you really mean it. The affirmation won't work if you are paying attention to any little voices in the background that say, "Yeah, right. Like that will ever happen." We all have an inner critic who talks to us, puts in its two cents, and adds doubt. Pay attention as you say affirmations. Do you hear other thoughts, maybe doubting or self-critical thoughts?

If you are using affirmations, be sure that your subconscious mind understands what you are saying. Remember, the subconscious mind is like a small child. It only thinks in the present tense, the here and now. It doesn't understand the future and it doesn't hear negative words, it only hears the rest.

Let me illustrate with a couple of examples. If you say, "I don't want so much pain," your body hears, "I want so much pain." If you say, "I don't want to feel anxious," your body hears, "I want to feel anxious." Always begin by focusing on what you want. Some people don't know what they want. However, if you know what you don't want, that helps you identify what you do want.

In the examples above, think of what you'd rather have instead of the pain. Maybe it includes words like "comfort," "energy" or "relaxed." The statement could then be, "I am comfortable and have all the energy I need." Rather than feeling anxious, you may want to feel calm and relaxed. So, "I feel calm and relaxed" is in present tense, avoids negative words and focuses on what you want.

There are several ways we can add power and an extra punch to our affirmations by incorporating some additional techniques while saying them. Affirmations are most effective if we can feel like we are already there. They are most powerful if we say them aloud. Additionally, saying an affirmation often and with feeling is more effective. Sometimes people say their affirmations don't work because nothing has changed. I ask them how often they say them and they tell me they've said them a lot, at least twenty times. Then I ask them what percentage of the time do they have negative thoughts or think about what they don't want. More often than not, those thoughts about what they don't want have consumed much of their day. You don't want the negative thoughts, or the feelings of scarcity or lack, to have more power in your life than what you want.

Louise Hay, author of inspirational, self-help books (www.louisehay.com), developed a technique called mirror work. In her book, *You Can Heal Your Life*, she illustrates this technique for affirmations. You look at yourself in the mirror, looking deeply into your eyes, and say your affirmations aloud, as though you really mean them. We don't often truly look at ourselves in the mirror, let alone look at ourselves eye-to-eye, coming from a place of compassion.

I have done this with patients in the office. I have them repeat a statement over and over. Initially, it's difficult. They might have difficulty looking at themselves in the mirror; it's foreign to them. Once they've done it for a little while, their words start to sound different. They start to sound more confident and begin to believe more in what they are saying. There truly is power in words, and looking yourself in the eye while looking in the mirror makes the affirmation more potent.

When I was recovering from my car accident and my brain was healing, I would look in the mirror and talk to myself every time I would use the bathroom. I would say, "Bonnie, I am so glad your brain is getting better and better every day." Soon, I started saying "every minute of every day," and I felt happy and confident. I knew my brain was healing quickly and

I would be even better than I was before. I didn't have any doubt, and my affirmation became stronger and more enthusiastic every day. Now, I have no research to back up the belief that my affirmations and positive thoughts enhanced my healing, but I choose to believe they did.

Writing down your affirmations is another way to add energy. The power of the written word is truly amazing. When writing your affirmations, remember to use present tense and avoid negative words. Add color and images if you like. You should feel good and believe that these are true even if you are not experiencing them now. Focus on what you want and feel as though you are already there. Remember, the feeling is more important than the words.

Some people have sticky notes all over their house with written affirmations. They say affirmations don't work because nothing has changed. I ask them how much of the time they feel good about the statement and feel as though they already have it. I ask them how much they believe, and it's the feeling that is usually lacking. Words are just words, whether they are verbalized or written. Saying affirmations while you are relaxed state of inner focus helps bring the good stuff to the top of the pile in your subconscious mind. Add as many senses as you can; add sound or music or images. There may be particular scents that remind you of a time you felt good, and it can bring back that feeling. The aroma of baked bread, fresh from the oven, reminds me of being a little girl at my grandma's house and how special and loved she always made me feel. The more senses you activate during affirmation work, the more powerful it will be. Vision boards can be a great way to put visuals to your affirmation. A vision board is simply a visual representation of the things you want to have, be, or do in your life. It consists of a poster or foam board filled with pictures, drawings and/or writing of the things you want in your life or the things you want to become.

Multi-media tools to use with affirmations also are very effective. I have come upon this in the past year or so and I have to admit that I have never before seen anything like it. Using your computer, you download images and write affirmations on the images, and you can create your own slide show and put it to music. It's very easy to do. There is software that is both free and for purchase. Animoto (www.animoto.com) and Mind Movies (www.mindmovies.com) are two ideal sources. I have used this and love watching the little movies I have made.

The Bridge in Our Brain

Remember when we talked about the two hemispheres of your brain, the right and left sides, and the band of fibers down the center that serves as the connection between them? Think of that connection as the bridge. When we are stressed, the bridge is closed and nothing gets through. However, if we cross our arms and ankles and breathe comfortably and deeply, it's like opening the bridge.

There is a natural crossing in our brain in which the right side of our brain operates the left side of our body and vice versa. When we cross our ankles and arms on the outside, we reinforce that crossing. What we are saying and consciously thinking is in the left hemisphere, and when the bridge is open, it is better able to travel to the right hemisphere. This allows us to connect with that subconscious mind much better. The right hemisphere, remember, is much more closely related to the subconscious mind.

Using positions that cross our arms and legs integrates our right and left hemispheres better. It's a great way to give affirmations more power and to help get to the subconscious mind. Remember, that's where everything is, and whatever is at the top of the stack is what drives our thoughts, feelings…and our life. Sitting in this way as you practice affirmations can be a great method to begin the process of shifting those subconscious beliefs. It's like priming the pump.

To use this technique, sit with your ankles crossed, arms out in front of you, palms facing outward as you did with the two-minute relaxation technique described earlier. Cross one arm over the other, whichever way is comfortable for you. Interlock your fingers and rest your arms in your lap. Repeat your affirmation over and over. You can say your affirmation out loud or silently to yourself. Remember to be in present tense and avoid the negative words. When you hear the statement change a bit, as if the accent is on a different part of the affirmation, it's a sign that the statement is going from the left hemisphere to the right hemisphere and reaching the subconscious mind.

PSYCH-K is a unique and direct way to identify and change subconscious beliefs that perpetuate old habits of thinking and behaving that you would like to change. It is a simple process that helps you communicate with your subconscious mind so you can change beliefs that limit you. You can learn more about this process or find a facilitator at www.dev.psych-k.com.

What Do I Subconsciously Believe?

So how do you know if your affirmation is something that you really believe at that subconscious level? Muscle testing, or kinesiology, is an easy way to find out. You don't need any special equipment. I believe it serves the same purpose as a lie-detector test. You can learn muscle testing yourself and this helps you acknowledge that you believe what you just said.

Let's use this example: "I feel calm and relaxed." If you say this to yourself as though you really mean it, your muscle will be strong if your subconscious mind agrees. However, if the subconscious mind doesn't agree with what you just said, it causes conflict in the two hemispheres of the brain and there is weakness in your muscles.

You may have experienced this muscle-testing technique before when a practitioner pushed on your arm when testing you for allergies or a supplement. You were asked to keep your arm straight to assess any weakness.

When you are using a statement or an affirmation and want to test if you really believe it, it is important to look downward as you are saying it; look at the floor or something below you. Looking downward puts your attention to the right hemisphere. The right hemisphere is where the emotions are and is most closely tied to our subconscious mind.

Muscle Testing Yourself

There are a few easy ways a person can do their own muscle testing. We use a smaller muscle as opposed to your arm, which is a bit awkward (see the options below). We will use some test statements first, and I recommend you do this each time you are working on testing an affirmation. This way you can feel what a weak muscle response feels like versus a strong muscle response.

For a test statement, you can simply say the word "yes" and then the word "no" and test each time you say it. You also can say something you know is true, like your name: "My name is (your name)." Now, test. Then use a name that isn't yours and has no meaning for you. "My name is (not your name)." Test again. Can you feel a difference? You also can use other true/false statements and/or a positive versus negative feeling and test that. There are many ways to do muscle testing on yourself. Here are a few. Find the one that works for you.

Option 1

Press together the pads of the thumb and index or pinky finger, forming an O-ring as shown in the picture. Interlock your two hands through these O-rings. (It should look like a chain link.) Focus your eyes downward, use your test statement, and note the amount of resistance when you try to pull your fingers apart.

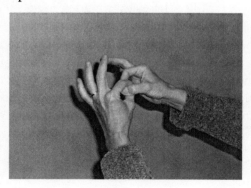

Option 2

Place your hand on your leg or some other surface, lift your index finger, and, while your eyes are focused downward, say your true and false statements. Gently push down on your raised index finger and feel the amount of resistance.

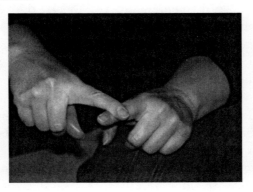

Option 3

Place the pads or tips of your thumb and index finger together, as in the picture. Take your other hand and, using your index finger, see how much resistance you feel when you try to separate your fingers.

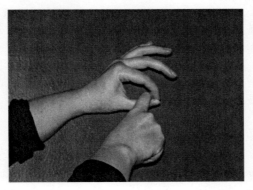

Option 4

While seated, cross one ankle over the opposite knee. Try to push it off with one hand. Notice the resistance.

Option 5

Stand up and keep your body relaxed. Say the true/false statements. Keep your eyes focused downward and really relax your body, then say your statement as though you really mean it. Your body will naturally sway forward or backward. If you are calm and relaxed enough to do this, your body will move. If you move forward, that is positive and means you believe what you just said. If your body sways backward, that is a negative response and means you don't believe what you just said.

When you are ready to muscle-test yourself with your statement, choose an option that works for you. Everyone is different. Use whatever statement you would like to test and one of the testing methods listed. Look downward, to be more in tune with the right hemisphere of your brain, where the emotions are. Say your statement as though you really mean it. When you say your statement, see how much resistance there is with whatever method you chose. It's a skill, like anything else, so it may take some practice. The more you practice, the more you will be in tune with your body.

Now let's practice. Think of something that makes you feel really happy, something you really like. Get that thought, that image, that memory firmly in your mind. Muscle-test yourself. How strong is the response? Most likely it will be strong.

Now, switch gears and think of something that you really don't like, something that makes you angry or sad, something that makes you feel icky or not well. Really get into the feeling and then muscle-test yourself again. Chances are you will have a different response. The muscle testing will be weaker. You can see how much energy we lose when we feel like this! No wonder why we feel so fatigued sometimes. When you use muscle testing, it's easy to see that having bad emotions or feelings zaps all of our energy.

I often relate muscle testing to that of a basketball player. There is usually one person on the team who can't make free throws. They can practice and practice and imagine getting the ball into that hoop all they want, but at the last split second, a part of them doesn't believe they can do it. There is a little bit of muscle weakness which throws off their shot and they don't make the free throw, usually coming up short. That shows muscle weakness because they didn't believe they could do it at a subconscious level.

Summary and Suggestions

We can control the world inside. Our thoughts and feelings shape our lives. A belief is just a thought you keep having; we all have limiting beliefs that can keep us stuck. Stress is a necessary part of life; how it affects us is up to us. Hypnosis happens more often than we think. Everything we have ever experienced is in our subconscious mind: the good, the bad, and the ugly. We should have the good stuff at the top.

- Take some quiet time and practice imagery. It is the back door to the subconscious mind.
- Take a mini-mental vacation.
- Notice how much of the day you have positive thoughts and feel good, and how much of the day you don't. Which is dominant?
- Daydream about the life you want and believe that it's possible.
- Make a list of the things you think about on a regular basis that don't make you feel good. This will give you an idea of what some of your limiting beliefs might be.
- Use affirmations and imagery to move life-enhancing beliefs to the top of the pile in your subconscious mind.
- Play around with the self-muscle testing techniques and find one that works for you. This is a way to discover what you believe at a subconscious level.

We make hundreds of choices every day and don't even think about it. Next, we'll examine how these choices affect our lives.

Third Key – We Have a Choice

"You cannot control what happens to you, but you can control your attitude toward what happens to you, and, in that, you will be mastering change rather than allowing it to master you."
~ Brian Tracy, personal development and motivational speaker

We are free to choose in our lives. That is a right we have as human beings. Sometimes, as adults, I think we forget that. Every thought, feeling and action is a choice. Just a millisecond before we have that thought or feeling, at some level we decide to have it. Usually it's at a subconscious level and we are not always aware of it. We make good choices when we value, love and accept ourselves unconditionally. When we are not eating right, exercising, resting well or taking time to relax, breathe, and just be, we may believe we are not worthy on some level. We have choice points in our lives every day; notice how you choose.

When faced with unpleasant circumstances in our lives, it's sometimes difficult to "choose" to feel good about the situation, but it is still our choice.

There is a story I often tell when using the Ericksonian Hypnosis Technique. It's about a famous tourist attraction in Hawaii. On the island of Maui, there is a popular activity called "taking the road to Hana." Many people who go to Maui take this journey. The road to Hana goes up a little mountainside; it's a twisty, winding road that is just gravel in some parts. People start early in the morning because it's pretty slow going. There are usually lots of cars on the road, and there is only one road to Hana. Depending on the season, there might be potholes in the road or it might be dusty. The bumpy, slow ride, with occasional dust coming through the car windows, irritates some people. Some cars go really slowly. It's impossible to pass anybody, so you have to stay behind any cars ahead of you. In some places the road is only one way, so you must stop and wait for the oncoming traffic to pass before you can continue.

It takes a long time to get to Hana, about two to three hours. When travelers finally arrive, they get out of the car, look around, and notice that Hana looks like every other Hawaiian village on Maui. At that moment, some of those people have an "ah-ha" moment, an epiphany, and they realize Hana isn't really the attraction. It's the road.

Life is kind of that like that – it's a journey, not a destination.

It takes a long time to get to Hana, so travelers are hungry for lunch. They stop and eat in the restaurant, maybe look in the shops before they head back down the mountain. They get back in their car and set back down the mountainside, back to their hotels and homes. This time, however, for those people who had that epiphany on the top of that mountain, the trip is a little different. As they're driving, they notice the red and yellow hibiscus flowers in the ditches. They smell the blooming plumeria trees in the field next to the road. They drive a little further and hear water running. They look over and see a little waterfall right alongside the road. All those things were there on the way to Hana, they just didn't notice them.

Perhaps on the way up, they noticed the potholes, the slow traffic and the dust through the car windows. They didn't see the beauty that was there. Before you know it, the travelers are at the base of the mountain. The trip seemed much shorter and was much more enjoyable.

What Do You Choose to See?

What types of things do you notice in life, on your journey? Do you notice the potholes in your life, the slow traffic? Or do you notice the flowers, the fragrant smells and the waterfalls along the roadside? It really is all about choice and how we choose to see the world. Our experiences, beliefs and thoughts change this point of view. I bet the lives of some of those people who had that epiphany at the top of that mountain are never quite the same. They may see more flowers, smell more fragrances, notice more sounds and see the beauty in their lives.

How do you see the world?

We all veer off the path – that's human nature – so just recognize it, acknowledge those feelings, and choose to feel a bit better. You don't have to feel great, just better. When you feel better, it's a bit like climbing a ladder, but in this instance, rather than climbing to the next rung, you reach for the next better thought, and so on.

Your brain doesn't know the difference between real and imagined, so tell your story the way you want it to be, not necessarily the way it is at the moment. Pretend as though you are already where you want to be in your life, and you'll get back on the road again. Recognize that your life is not the same as it used to be, it may be better. It's all about how you look at it!

How we choose to react is up to us; no one can choose our reaction for us and no one can take our reaction away from us. There are a lot of "so-what" types of issues we encounter every day. Often they are not that significant, although they may seem to be at the time. But, really, usually nobody is dying, it's not the end of the world, and chances are we won't even think it's important ten years from today.

Notice the So-What Issues

How often do you get frustrated or upset about something? And in these situations, how many times has someone died or something so disastrous happened that your life was in danger? Few things in life truly have a significant negative consequence. Most things we can fix, choose again or make amends. It's the chronic little stressors in our lives that cause us the most harm. Most people do just fine in a true emergency, maybe even better than they thought they would. It's the everyday irritations that make life difficult.

How many times do you say, "So what," and let it go right then and there? I think we don't say "so what" enough in our lives. Sometimes I hear people say, "Oh well," and that's great, too. However, I think saying "so what" gives extra punch and feels more empowering.

It's the letting-go part that many of us have trouble with, myself included. I find if I say "so what," it's a bit easier to let go. In many situations, it's good to ask ourselves, "What's the worst that could happen?" Will this be an issue five or ten years from now? Did anybody die? Will this one little event change my whole life in a big way? Will I even remember this? If we are not able to let go of little "so-what" issues, they may affect our lives negatively for a long time.

I have known people who missed family weddings, experienced deteriorating physical issues, became ill, or severed relationships and suffered loss largely because they couldn't let go and move on. Feelings such as anger and frustration are not bad or negative, they are just feelings. We should acknowledge them, but then we need to let them go.

Take something that happened to you recently. Maybe it was something someone said, or something you didn't complete the way you wanted, or maybe you didn't have the house clean when someone stopped by. Whatever happened, ask yourself these three questions, and answer yes or no:

1. Is my life in danger right now?
2. Is the life of my loved one in danger right now?
3. Will I really think this is an important moment in my life ten years from now.

If you answered "no" to all three of those questions, or certainly the first two, chances are it's a so-what issue. There are few things in life that we can't undo and fix. Often people believe that what is done is done, and we can't fix it. That is true sometimes, but during most situations we can undo, apologize or make a different decision. We can change our reaction; remember, it's our choice and no one else's. Ask yourself, "What's the worst that can happen?" So, company is coming and you didn't get the house completely cleaned. What's the worst that could happen? Are they going to walk into your house, look around and quickly leave because you didn't clean as well as you would have liked? People joke about having a bad hair day, but does anyone else even notice? I really doubt it. "So-what" issues cause a lot of stress in our lives, and we don't have to allow it.

I like to make a game out of this for patients. "Tammy" and I were talking about the "So-What" game a while ago. I asked her to keep track of so-what issues and ask herself the three questions. I saw her a couple of weeks later and she said, "Bonnie, you will never guess what happened." She went on to tell me that for the first time in her adult life, she was able to use a public restroom successfully. She is in her fifties, but she had never been able to use a public restroom, as she was too self-conscious. She told me she was sitting in the stall, had to go, and knew there was somebody in the stall next to her. She remembered the "So-What" game. She asked herself the three questions and thought to herself, "so what?" She was amazed that such a simple thing could change her life. It was a limiting belief she had carried with her and had limited her all her life.

How many "so-what" issues do you struggle with every day? How many times do you say "so what" throughout the day? It can be a fun exercise. You might be surprised how this simple little phrase can change your life!

We also tend to make things worse than they are by being too critical of ourselves. In his book, *Buddha's Brain,* Rick Hanson, PhD, a neuropsychologist, (www.rickhanson.net) uses a metaphor from the Buddha about throwing darts. The first dart is the event that happens, and the other dart or darts are all the thoughts we have after it happens. Say you pull your car to the wrong side of the gas pump and you think, "I am so stupid. I always forget that, and now I have to drive around and find another pump. I am in a hurry and now I'm going to be late." We react to the situation, and throw the second and third dart. It's the additional darts we throw that make the situation worse and cause us to have more feelings of negativity.

Business consultant and personal development coach Bob Proctor (www.bobproctor.com) talks about three guidelines to follow no matter what happens in your life. This was something he had heard at a Michael Beckwith presentation. They were so profound when I first heard them that I wrote them down while listening to his lecture:

1. It is what it is; accept it.
2. Harvest the good from the event/situation.
3. Forgive and let go of the rest.

Seems simple, right? The third guideline, letting go of the rest, is often the hardest. The problem is that we often get stuck and can't let go of a bad situation. We hang onto things and let them fester. Remember, whatever we focus our attention on grows. Detaching from the outcome can be challenging. I see so many people who live in the past; they aren't able to let go of some negative or traumatic event. It's a choice and no one can choose for us – that's our right and our privilege. We get to choose what we feel, what we hang on to, and from what we detach.

Some of the tools in this book may help you let go of some of the issues holding you back. Harvest the good, forgive and let go of the rest. If you can detach from the outcome, it makes things so much better and things usually will go the way you want them to.

Sometimes we need a place to deposit our unwanted thoughts and feelings, a place that will contain them for us. Imagine a repository for issues, like a box, or using the earth as a garbage disposal. This is different from stuffing your feelings. An imaginary repository lets you acknowledge your feeling and choose to put it away or let it go. If you are not in a place emotionally where you can let it go, a least put it away for a while. "Mary" created a physical box to put her worries in, and her daughter helped her by decorating the box with drawings of smiley faces and flowers. Mary allowed herself to worry about something for just a minute or two, and then she put the worry in the box. The rule was she couldn't think about it for twenty-four hours. At that point, if necessary, she could take it out and think about it again for another two minutes. This technique kept her from worrying all day about something.

Another technique is to imagine using the earth as a receptacle, a garbage disposal of sorts, to dispose of all the negative things you don't want anymore. You can go through the motions of throwing something away, image seeing it fall down into the center of the earth, where it can be recycled into better thoughts.

Journaling is also a great way to get rid of negative thoughts and express your intense emotions. Write down your feelings and get them out. You can write a nasty-gram to someone that you will never send, but it will make you feel better. Creating some sort of a ceremony or ritual to let go of the content of those journals or letters is powerful. You can tear pages into little pieces and thrown them away. You can burn them, dispose of them somehow, and bid them good riddance. These days with cell phones, especially the ones you can wear in your ear, no one knows if you are talking to yourself or someone on the phone when you have a conversation by yourself. You can get your feelings out while you are alone in the car. Nowadays, you won't even get a strange look from anyone. It will make you feel so much better.

Choose to Eat Well

We have a choice in how we care for our bodies, how we eat, what kinds of foods we eat and how much water we drink. Those are all choices we make many times a day. Sometimes we overindulge, and then we feel guilty. Know that feeling guilty is unnecessary. So, you overindulged. It happens! The 80/20 rule applies here. If you choose wisely 80 percent of the time, generally you will be fine. Let go of the other 20 percent.

It is healthy to eat a diet that is low in saturated fat, processed foods and refined sugars. If you shop around the outside of the grocery store, generally that's where you'll find the healthier, fresher foods. You find processed foods in the inner aisles of the grocery store. As you walk up and down the aisles, notice how many foods can sit there for a long time without spoiling. If you pick up a bottle, can or a box from a shelf, look at the ingredients. Are there words that are really long and difficult to pronounce? That's probably not a good food to eat. If you look at the container and the expiration date is two to three years in the future, that's not a good food to eat, either. Manufacturers add a lot of chemicals to those foods to give them a long shelf life.

Anything that is not good for your brain isn't good for your body or well-being, either. Chemicals are not good for our brains. Try to limit the amount of processed foods you eat. Most people realize that going to a fast-food restaurant regularly is not healthy. However, many people use lots of pre-made foods like canned and boxed foods, and frozen dinners, all of which are primarily processed foods. Those also aren't good for you. I urge you to check out how many chemicals you are getting with these foods.

Moderation is the key. Balancing protein, carbohydrates and fats throughout the day stabilizes your blood sugar and actually keeps you satisfied longer. Whether it is a meal or just a snack, make sure to balance the protein, carbohydrates and fats. Fluctuations in your blood sugar throughout the day may cause you to feel fatigued, weak or worsen pain issues (physical and emotional). It can zap your energy. Eat foods that nourish you and help maintain a stable blood sugar. A stable blood sugar is about 80 to 140 mg/dL, depending on the time of day and whether it's before or after a meal. The body quickly metabolizes carbohydrates, whereas proteins and fats take longer. This evens out your blood sugar levels. Carbs make your blood sugar increase more than proteins or fats.

Spikes in blood sugar cause your pancreas to produce and release more insulin. Our body naturally wants balance, so it will always have a reaction to any changes in an attempt to maintain that balance. The release of insulin causes the blood sugar to fall. This effect is most important at night. Suppose you eat ice cream or popcorn in the evening, and then go to bed. Your blood sugar spikes because of these carbohydrates. To maintain balance, the pancreas secretes insulin to fix it. The blood sugar then falls. But in this case, you are sleeping and won't be eating for a while. Remember, your body wants balance; it wants a normal blood sugar. So, to fix this, the adrenal glands – the small glands above your kidneys – start releasing cortisol.

Cortisol sometimes is called the stress hormone. Cortisol is also like the drug prednisone in that it will increase your blood sugar without you eating any food. The adrenal glands make extra cortisol to get your blood sugar back to a normal range. If your body has to release a lot of cortisol to increase your blood sugar, you may not sleep well. Besides, you don't need all that extra cortisol. Remember it's also a stress hormone. Too much cortisol hinders digestion and metabolism, increases blood pressure, decreases your immune response, and causes stomach disorders and weight gain, especially around the midsection. If you have a lot of stress in your life and you eat carbohydrates in the evening, you may be dealing with high cortisol levels. I am not saying you shouldn't eat ice cream or popcorn in the evening, just don't have it by itself. Balance your snack with some protein and fat. Ice cream has fat but little protein, so add some. Same thing with popcorn. Balancing your foods, especially at night, may help your sleep.

"Nicole" didn't sleep well. She routinely ate canned fruit every night before going to bed. Fruit is good for us, but it's still just a carbohydrate with little fat and protein. She changed her evening snack, adding protein, and found she slept better. There are lots of reasons people don't sleep well, but for Nicole, just changing her evening snack helped. Her blood sugar was more stable and her body didn't need to fix the low blood sugar by secreting more cortisol. Thus, she could sleep better.

Eating a healthy diet with lots of fruits and vegetables is a good idea. I always tell people to eat in Technicolor. Most beige, brown and white foods are not good for us; the rare exception being cauliflower. There is much more nutritional value in blueberries, the red and orange foods, and the dark, leafy green vegetables.

There isn't much protein in fruit. A few almonds or walnuts add enough protein, keep you satisfied longer and will stabilize your blood sugar. Eight almonds are considered a serving, so it doesn't take a lot to add some protein. Almonds and walnuts also are really good sources of omega-3s – the good fats.

Eating enough, but not too much protein to keep you satisfied from meal to meal, is helpful as well. In the United States, people don't have trouble eating enough protein. The problem is that we generally eat it all at one time rather than spacing it throughout the day. For example, an average portion should be about the size of a deck of cards. We generally eat more than a portion-size serving in the U.S.

Don't skip meals. It is true when you hear that breakfast is the most important meal of the day. Breakfast is the first time you will be eating since your last meal the previous day. Overnight is the longest time that we go between meals, and your blood sugar can become really low. Breakfast need not be bacon and eggs. It just needs to be something that balances the protein, carbs and fats. Eat within two hours or so of getting up in the morning.

Eating foods with a lower glycemic index will prevent hunger and keep your blood sugar nice and stable. Keeping processed foods to a minimum is a good guideline. I often say that if God made it, eat it; if not, maybe you shouldn't. If you can afford organic foods, that's even better. Decrease the amount of trans-fatty acids found in items such as fried food, bakery, chips, cookies, vegetable oil and margarine. Trans-fats increase inflammation and are just not good for us. Look for zero trans-fats on the label.

Increase the amount of good fats such omega-3 fatty acids, which include things like fish oil and flax seed oil. Omega-3s protect our heart and brain. Anything that protects your brain will help you think and feel better.

The Importance of Water

Drink enough water each day. I can't stress the importance of this enough. I usually recommend about eight glasses of water a day unless you can't drink that much water because of a health reason. Our bodies are 70 percent to 80 percent water, and it doesn't take much to create just a 2 percent drop. This drop will cause some daytime fuzziness and is the number one cause of afternoon fatigue. It can worsen emotional and physical pain, and can cause memory and cognitive issues. I encourage people to water their brains. If you have a 2 percent drop in body water, your body is going to steal water from wherever it can get it, and the brain is one of those places. It's that balance concept again. The body wants balance and will do what it needs to maintain it. Imagine what houseplants look like when you forget to water them. They look kind of droopy, right? Well, our brains need watering, too.

How to get more water in your diet:
1. Drink water with meals in addition to other beverages.
2. Have a glass of water every time you use the restroom.
3. Have a glass of water when you get up in the morning and at bedtime.
4. Carry bottled water with you (at work, in the car, etc.)

Everything in Moderation

It's good to think in terms of everything in moderation. If you drink alcohol, do so in moderation. Besides, it's like liquid candy. There are lots of empty calories in alcohol. Moderation for women is one normal size drink per day, and for men it is two per day.

The same goes for caffeine. Too much caffeine can cause unwanted side effects including anxiety, restlessness, irritability and sleep problems. So, how much is too much? Not everyone tolerates caffeine the same. Most sources say that 200 mg to 300 mg of caffeine a day is OK for most people, unless you are one of those who doesn't tolerate it well. More than 200 mg to 300 mg a day usually causes problems.

Caffeine mildly stimulates the nervous and cardiovascular systems. It affects the brain and results in decreased fatigue and increased attentiveness, so a person is able to think more clearly and work harder. It also increases the heart rate, blood flow, respiratory rate and metabolic rate for several hours. If you have anxiety issues, caffeine may make that worse. When taken before bedtime, caffeine can interfere with falling asleep and/or staying asleep.

Even when withdrawing moderate amounts of caffeine for eighteen to twenty-four hours, we may feel symptoms such as headache, fatigue, irritability, depression and poor concentration. Anyone who has stopped ingesting caffeine cold turkey will confirm that it wasn't a pleasant experience. Coffee has the highest caffeine content, but caffeine is also high in certain sodas and teas. The exception is non-caffeinated herbal tea. To give you an example, a five-ounce cup of coffee contains 100 mg to 130 mg of caffeine. Now, who has a five-ounce cup? Most cups these days are eight ounces or larger. An average eight-ounce cup of coffee contains 95 mg to 200 mg. One can of dark soda, such as a cola, contains about 50 mg of caffeine.

If possible, avoid or limit soft drinks. Diet sodas are the biggest issue with soft drinks. Moderation is the key here. Aspartame, sold under the name NutraSweet, is a chemical found in most diet sodas. It is detrimental to our brain and our general health. This is especially dangerous if you have pain issues, as it can make these issues worse. It doesn't matter if you have depression, mood issues or physical pain, the effect is the same. When diet soda is sitting in a glass or can, it isn't doing too much damage. However, as soon as we drink it, our body temperature warms it and changes the chemical composition of aspartame to something similar to formaldehyde, which can really do a number on our bodies. Morticians use formaldehyde to embalm people after they die. Does that sound like something you want in your body or your brain? Again, moderation is the key here.

"Sara" went to the doctor because she thought something was terribly wrong with her. She was not feeling well, was depressed, fatigued, and had physical pain issues. The doctor diagnosed her with fibromyalgia, depression and possible chronic fatigue. He prescribed some medication and sent her home. A friend noticed Sara drank a lot of diet cola and encouraged her to try stopping that to see what would happen. It took Sara about three weeks or so to wean herself from the diet soda. She went from six cans a day to eliminating the soda completely. A couple of weeks later, all her symptoms went away. She didn't have fibromyalgia, chronic fatigue or depression. She had aspartame poisoning.

It really doesn't take much aspartame to create a negative effect. The scariest part is that many foods contain aspartame. There are also several other soft drinks that have artificial sweeteners in them. It behooves us to look at labels.

"Scott" had an even more dramatic story. Scott was very ill. He had developed chronic pain and depression. He had to quit work and was confined to a wheelchair. He drank a lot of diet cola and decided to try eliminating it. He took a few weeks to slowly wean himself. After a while, his symptoms improved, he didn't need the wheelchair, and he began taking less pain medication. Now, he feels better and is enjoying his life again.

Soda in moderation is not harmful. Personally, I would rather have the sugar than the chemicals. If you have regular soda with sugar, be sure to eat something with it to balance your blood sugar. As discussed before, you need to add some protein and fat to the carbohydrates that are in the soda. The same is true for fruit juices.

Finally, it's obviously not good to smoke, chew tobacco or expose yourself to unnecessary chemicals. Chemicals of any kind are not good for our brain. That includes chemicals we inhale, like pesticides, vapors from household products and paint supplies, and so on. Anything that's not good for our brain is not good for our bodies. Whether it's chronic physical pain or depression, chemicals can make things worse.

Vitamins are Good Insurance

Our lives today are so busy. We don't often have time to eat well or sit down for a meal with the family. Even if people eat well – and not many people do – I usually recommend a quality multi-vitamin/mineral supplement with a good amount of magnesium and Vitamin D. Our everyday foods just don't contain the nutrients they did a hundred years ago due to decades of commercial soil fertilization, which has depleted much of the nutrients over time.

Vitamins and minerals strengthen our immune system, increase our metabolism and give us more energy. They also help our brain function by increasing memory and concentration. Take a quality multivitamin/mineral supplement twice a day; otherwise, it's like eating food just once a day and then waiting another twenty-four hours to get more nutrition. Nutritional supplements are regulated by the FDA as a food, and therefore do not have the same manufacturing guidelines as over-the-counter or prescription medicines. It takes effort to check out the quality of a particular product. There are a few companies in the United States that manufacture their products to "pharmaceutical grade," meaning the company voluntarily follows the same requirements the FDA has in place for over-the-counter and prescription drugs.

Look for these things in a good multivitamin/mineral:
- It should have a full spectrum of vitamins and minerals.
- It should absorb well in your body. Bioavailability refers to how well the cells of your body absorb the vitamins/minerals.
- Drop the multivitamin into a glass of water and see how long it takes to dissolve. A good product will dissolve in a couple of hours and not take all day.
- Chelated minerals usually absorb better because they are bound to something organic, like an amino acid.
- Look for the USP (United States Pharmacopeia) symbol. The USP provides assurance that the supplement is pure, safe and potent.
- The definition of RDA (Recommended Dietary Allowance) is the minimum requirements to sufficiently prevent deficiency problems, like beriberi (a deficiency of thiamine) and pellagra (a deficiency of niacin and protein). This is not the same as containing optimal amounts. Look for high percentages (even more than 100 percent) of RDA on the label. Remember that RDA is the minimum requirement, not the optimal amount.

The Comparative Guide to Nutritional Supplements, by Lyle MacWilliam (www.comparativeguide.com) is a good resource and scores many multivitamins based on their quality and bioavailability.

Magnesium: The Relaxation Mineral

Magnesium is our body's "relaxation" mineral. If we have enough, we feel calmer, sleep well, have more energy and generally feel better. Magnesium is involved in more than three hundred enzymatic reactions in our body. Consequently, it affects a lot of things. Many of us are deficient in magnesium. Magnesium is nearly lost in the processing of packaged and fast foods. Certain medications, supplemental iron, high-protein diets and high doses of calcium block its absorption. Calcium is stronger than magnesium, so when we take calcium without additional magnesium, we lose magnesium as the calcium pushes it out of the cells.

Physical and emotional stresses also cause magnesium loss. Who doesn't have some sort of stress in their life? If you suffer from chronic physical or emotional pain issues, you are stressed! Even extreme athletes, like marathon runners and long-distance cyclists, lose magnesium due to the physical stress of their strenuous exercise. As magnesium leaves the cell, calcium jumps in to replace it and the cell contracts. How do you think you'll feel when your cells are all tight and contracted? Not so good. Most magnesium research is conducted outside the United States, since research in the U.S. is costly and the pharmaceutical industry funds most of it. Not surprisingly, little money and attention is given to research not related to drugs.

Magnesium-rich foods include spinach and other green vegetables, pumpkin seeds, nuts, legumes, halibut, unprocessed grains, kelp and sea salt, just to name a few. Remember, foods do not have the nutritional value they did a hundred years ago due to poor soil from decades of commercial fertilization. I recommend eating a healthy diet with magnesium-rich foods and taking a good multivitamin/mineral with an adequate amount of magnesium (about 300 mg). If you take a calcium supplement, it should have magnesium in it as well. Remember, calcium is stronger than magnesium and it pushes out the magnesium. Calcium also tends to have a constipating effect while magnesium can cause loose stools at high doses. If you take them in the same supplement, you avoid these side effects.

Magnesium oxide is not the best form of magnesium. Unfortunately, it's what you often find. Only a small percentage of magnesium oxide absorbs into our bodies. Instead, find a calcium supplement that contains a better form of magnesium, like citrate, malate, glycinate or taurate, or magnesium oxide mixed with another form.

If you're on blood pressure medication, monitor your blood pressure, as these supplements may result in the need for less medication. Do not take extremely high doses of magnesium if you have kidney failure, an excessively slow heart rate, bowel obstruction or myasthenia gravis.

Omega-3 – Fish Oil

Omega-3s are sometimes referred to as the good fats. They benefit us in many ways by protecting our heart, our brain, and just about everything in between. If looking for fish oil or omega-3 at the store, be sure to look for two things on the label:
- It should say mercury-free or purified, because fish oil is made from fish from the ocean. There's a lot of garbage in the ocean, and you want to make sure the manufacturer purified the fish oil.
- Look at the active ingredients. You should see DHA (docosahexaenoic acid) and EPA (eicosapentaenoic acid).

Another option for omega-3 is flax seed ALA (alpha-linolenic acid), which is a major benefit to vegetarians who don't consume fish but require omega-3 in their healthy diet. Flax seed is made from flax, a plant that's been with us for thousands of years. Seeds need to be ground to get to the oil.

Vitamin D: The Sunshine Vitamin

Vitamin D is essential for our bodies. There has been a lot in the news about the benefits of vitamin D and that many of us are deficient. A simple blood test can be done by your health-care provider to determine your level of vitamin D. Vitamin D is essential for strong bones, mental well-being and the immune system, to name a few. Getting out in the sunshine is the best way to obtain vitamin D. Don't you feel better if you are out in the sun? You don't have to sun bathe, just expose your forearms and face. According to the Vitamin D Council, (www.vitamindcouncil.org), when in the sun, Caucasians produce about 10,000 units of vitamin D in about half an hour.

Sunscreen blocks the absorption of vitamin D. I advise spending twenty to thirty minutes outside without sunscreen (but don't do it when the sun is strong, like at noon). Then go back inside and put on some sunscreen. It takes awhile to absorb and produce vitamin D, so don't shower immediately after coming inside as it will wash it away. People with dark skin need a longer exposure time, up to six times longer. In the winter months, especially in northern climates, it is not as easy to get into the sun. Vitamin D-3 supplements are helpful in the winter.

Are You Sensitive to Foods?

Many of us are sensitive to foods. It's not a true allergy, but some foods cause us distress, nonetheless. The elimination diet is still the gold standard to see if there are certain foods that worsen your symptoms. If you think some of the foods you are eating are causing you issues, follow the directions below to do an elimination diet.

- Look at what is in your normal diet.
- Eliminate foods you think may be potential triggers for your symptoms for at least one month.
- Bring the foods back, one at a time, leaving a week in between each added food.
- Keep a diary of your symptoms; note any changes.
- Decide if there are foods that trigger your symptoms.
- If a certain food group or a specific food makes your symptoms worse, avoid it for at least four to six months before slowly reintroducing it. See if your body can tolerate it with a gradual increase in amount.

Of course, you want to nourish your mind as well as your body. Food is for our physical body what thoughts and feelings are for our minds, our mental body. Take time to nourish your mind through a variety of ways: meditation, imagery and daydreaming, laughing, thinking positively, feeling good and being thankful. Gratitude is extremely important for your physical and emotional health.

Choose to Get Moving

We can choose to move our bodies. Exercise is good for us. It's important that you exercise by doing something you enjoy. If you go to the gym and you hate every minute of it, it is not doing you any good. If you are happier being goofy, jumping on a trampoline or dancing in your house when nobody is watching, do it. You need to feel good while you are exercising. Don't see it as a punishment or a penance that you must do. See it as something you enjoy and something that is your choice to do. Exercise that you enjoy feeds your spirit as well as your body.

We all know exercise is good for us, but how good is it? Moving our body is healthy for every part of us, even our brain, and we don't have to run a marathon to see the benefit. At least thirty minutes of exercise on most days of the week will help, and it doesn't have to be all at one time. We can even break it up to fit it into our day. Just walking to the car, taking the stairs, or getting up from the desk or the couch every hour helps. Even housework counts as exercise!

I am a migraine sufferer and I have found that exercising helps reduce my migraines more than anything else does. While all the other things I do help to keep the migraines under control, regular exercise makes the biggest difference.

Moving our bodies and engaging in regular exercise helps us lose weight, reduce stress, relieve symptoms of depression and anxiety, and decrease our risk of heart disease and certain types of cancer. It also gives us more energy, helps us sleep better, and improves our quality of life. Exercise helps prevent and improve a number of health problems, including high blood pressure, diabetes and arthritis. There are many studies on exercise and how it helps increase bone density, and strengthen our heart and lungs. Research on anxiety, depression and exercise shows the psychological and physical benefits of exercise also help reduce anxiety, improve our mood and decrease symptoms of depression.

We feel good when we finish exercising. I don't always want to start exercising, but I always feel good when I'm done. What many people don't realize is how beneficial exercise is for our memory as well as our concentration. We think better! Certainly, mental stimulation improves brain function and actually protects against cognitive decline, but so does physical exercise. So if you play games like Sudoku and other brainteasers to improve your brain power, don't forget to move your body or you could be missing out on the brain benefits.

Here are some general exercise guidelines:
- Exercise at least thirty minutes most, if not all, days of the week.
- Exercise with a buddy.
- Create an exercise routine.
- Do exercise you enjoy; do it for you.
- If using indoor exercise equipment during inclement weather, keep the equipment in a place you enjoy.
- Consider joining a health club. Everybody there is exercising, so it can be an added motivator.
- Consider hiring a trainer to develop an individualized plan for you. Some health clubs offer this as a free service.
- Get outside as much as possible, even in winter.

- Tai chi, Qi-gong, and yoga can help with balance, strength and flexibility, and are great for the mind, as well.
- Incorporating several smaller segments of exercise into your daily routine is as beneficial as one block of time daily.
- Walk more by parking at the end of the parking lot.
- Wear a pedometer.
- Take the stairs rather than the elevator.

Choose to Give Your Body Rest

We can choose to sleep well, believe it or not. I know many people have sleep disturbances and insomnia issues and they certainly are not choosing to have trouble sleeping, but on a subconscious level, they may not believe they can sleep and get frustrated. Or they find themselves waking in the middle of the night thinking, "Oh great, I'm awake again." Perhaps they have a busy mind and find themselves thinking about what happened that day or all the things they need to do the next day. Sometimes when we worry or can't settle our mind, we can't sleep. The ANTs (Automatic Negative Thoughts) are running wild. There may be something subconsciously, some limiting belief or previous experience, keeping them from a restful sleep.

We can choose to have good sleep hygiene. We can choose to wind down before we go to bed and be in the right frame of mind to sleep. We can choose to relax our bodies before we go to bed; however, we can't expect magic -- that we will instantly fall asleep. We can choose to fall asleep with good thoughts. How many of us go to bed thinking about the things we didn't do, the things we have to do, the things we are worried about, or whatever didn't go well that day? Those thoughts consume much of the time right before sleep. Yet it is a choice. Choose to focus on something positive, recall a favorite memory, remember a time when you really had fun, a morning that you enjoyed sleeping in and woke up feeling rested. Those are all better thoughts than thinking, "I am never going to fall asleep tonight."

Sometimes stress and emotions keep us from sleeping, as well. If we fall asleep thinking of stressful things that happened or might happen, sometimes we have bad dreams or nightmares. It's our subconscious mind working things out while we sleep. Certainly get help from a professional if you think you may need a sleep-disturbance evaluation. Some people with sleep disturbance or insomnia issues need to be checked out medically, so be sure to take care of yourself and get some help.

Here are a few things that will help you fall asleep easily at night.
- Don't go to bed if you are not ready for bed.
- Don't work on the computer or watch TV before bed, as both can be too engaging.
- Take some time to disengage and unwind before trying to sleep. Calm down and relax about an hour and a half before you go to bed. If you plan to get to bed at 10 p.m., don't still be doing the laundry, vacuuming or working on the computer after 8:30 p.m.
- Beware, a really good book or movie also might keep you engaged and not prepared for sleep. Don't watch an intense drama, thriller, or even the news just before bed. "Steve" had trouble sleeping as a teenager. He read a dictionary at night to fall asleep because it was hard to become completely interested in the dictionary. His mother often would find him in bed with a huge dictionary over his chest. He had fallen asleep that way. Doing something boring is better than doing something engaging.
- Create a ritual or habit. Brushing your teeth, washing your face, combing your hair, whatever you do in the evening, can become a routine. When you do these things in the same order and same way, it retrains your brain to expect that going to bed and sleeping comes next in the sequence. Going through this sequence of events every night makes it easier to sleep.
- Avoid reading, eating or watching TV in bed. Over the course of time, this gives your body the wrong message. It tells your body that it's time to watch TV (or whatever) when you go to bed. If you want to read or watch TV in your bedroom, sit in a chair instead.
- Strategies such as going to bed only when you're sleepy and getting out of bed after fifteen to twenty minutes if you're unable to sleep, returning to bed only when you feel ready, have been shown to re-establish the psychological connection between the bedroom and sleeping.
- Sometimes meditation, listening to relaxing music or doing imagery can be a helpful in falling asleep.

I have included a guided meditation script to help you sleep. Simply read the script slowly and record yourself or have someone read it or record it for you. This guided meditation audio also is available on my website (www.bonniegroessl.com).

Restful Sleep Guided Meditation

It's best to use this technique when you go to bed and are ready for sleep.

"To begin, get in a comfortable position, your favorite position in bed, and allow yourself to sink into the bed. Close your eyes and focus your attention on your breathing. Just breathing comfortably, in and out through your nose ... continuing to breathe in and out through the nose, feeling the air coming in through your nose and going down to your abdomen ... as you slowly exhale, let your abdomen relax and deflate, letting all tension and discomfort go with the out-breath. Feel the tension flowing from your body with each exhalation. As tension and discomfort leaves, you begin to relax. You're more comfortable.

"As you continue breathing, you may notice that you relax more and more with every breath. You may notice the muscles in your scalp and face begin to relax with every breath; your eyes become heavier, jaw relaxing, neck muscles loosening. Like a warm, comfortable, progressive wave of relaxation spreading down your body, leaving you more and more relaxed with every breath. ... This wave of relaxation is now spreading down to your shoulders, comfortable warm spreading feeling of total relaxation ... loose, limp muscles spreading down your arms, to your elbows ... all the way down to your wrists and hands ... allowing any remaining tension to flow out your fingertips. You may notice that you feel somewhat more relaxed than you did when you started ... you may even notice that as you continue to breathe, you will feel more and more relaxed ...

"As you continue to breathe ... your chest and upper back begin to loosen, relax ... loose, limp muscles ... down to your abdomen and lower back ... loosening, relaxing, becoming more and more relaxed with every breath. Loose, limp muscles, feeling comfortably heavy and warm ... down to your hips and thighs ... spreading down to your knees, ankles and feet ... allowing any remaining tension to flow out your toes ... Knowing that as you continue to breath, you will become even more relaxed with every breath.

"Now you imagine a staircase before you, see it in your mind's eye ... it may be a staircase you have seen before, or perhaps it's one that you just now imagined. This is a magical staircase that will take you to a deep, restful sleep ... Notice the details of this magical staircase. What does it look like? Is it

wood or some other material? Is there a handrail? If so, you can touch it, feel comfortable as you approach this magical staircase, for you know it will take you to a deep, restful slumber. There are ten steps, and you are at the top, step number ten. As you slowly go down the stairs, you will become more and more relaxed, sleepier and sleepier. Now you begin going down, from step number ten going to nine ... feeling more and more relaxed ... eight ... feeling more and more sleepy and comfortable ... seven ... feeling so comfortable and heavy ... six ... feeling more and more sleepy ... five ... thoughts seem to fade away as you drift off ... four ... feeling more and more relaxed, comfortable, and sleepy ... three ... drifting off, mind quiet ... two ... feeling more and more sleepy, heavier, relaxed, drifting off ... and one ... feeling so relaxed and sleepy. Your body feels so heavy, you can't even lift your arm, soooo relaxed ... soooo comfortably heavy and warm.

"Now you are at the bottom of the stairs and a wonderful, comfortable place for you to slumber awaits you ... a cushion of air gently floats you over to this very special place that allows you to have a deep, restful sleep, a deep restful sleep. This place may look familiar, perhaps this is somewhere you have been before, maybe a comfortable bed in your favorite place ... perhaps even from an earlier time ... or it may be something you just imagine now. Sink into the wonderful, supportive, safe cushion of peace that awaits you. You now allow your mind to stop thinking, worrying, or planning. Feel the airy support, allowing you to feel the lightness of sleep, that twilight between awake and asleep ... feel the complete peace and calmness that envelopes you. You feel so relaxed and calm and safe. You allow your mind to stop thinking, worrying, or planning.

"There is only time for deep, restful sleep, no worries or thoughts from the day ... only comfort, deep comfort and peace ... so quiet ... so restful, an now you allow your mind to stop, you allow your body to sleep, deeply and restfully, and you enjoy this deep, restful sleep that envelopes you. There are only feelings of peace and comfort ... enjoy ... enjoy the wonderful feeling of sleep as it comes to you ... feels so good, so good. And you know that you'll sleep deeply and restfully for as long as you want and only awaken when it's time to get up, feeling refreshed and ready for the new day. ... You know as you drift further into this deep, restful, comfortable sleep, that you will only awaken when you want to and you'll feel refreshed when it is time to get up for the day. So enjoy ... enjoy ... the deep, comfortable sleep and the wonderful feeling of being rested and ready for tomorrow."

Choose Self-Acceptance

A lot of people struggle with lack of self-acceptance or worthiness. It's the number one reason we make bad choices. Some people use the term self-esteem. I think self-esteem has gotten a bad rap in the past. We should all be able to accept ourselves as we are, at any point in time. We should value our body and our mind, and know that we are deserving. If we truly value our body and our mind, we will take good care of it, just as if it was a small child or a dear friend.

Most people take better care of other people than they do of themselves. Think about why that is. Is there a message you heard as a child or somewhere in your past? Do you have a limiting belief that you are not good enough? Do you believe others are more important than you? We all know people who seem to have it all together, who are extremely busy, always going, like the Energizer bunny. If we ask them for a favor, it doesn't matter how busy they are, they will find a way to do it. Sometimes this type of person values others more than they value themselves; they have trouble saying no and setting boundaries. No one is superhuman, and if these people continue in this mode, it may eventually catch up with them.

If this is an issue for you, know that it's OK to say no without guilt. Setting boundaries is necessary for your health and well-being. Some of the tools, like EFT or using affirmations, may help you deal with this. Certainly if you need help in that area, see a therapist or a counselor. Sometimes, just talking to somebody is helpful. Do you have someone you can talk to? Maybe it's a good friend, a spouse, or a family member. I often ask people if they have someone they can call at 3 a.m. if they need to. It's important that we all have that someone for support. It's also important that we accept who we are. Each of us is perfect in this moment. We all do the best we can with what we have right now. I encourage you to be as kind to yourself as you are to those you love.

Choose to Know You Are Important

When I see people in the office who suffer in some way, perhaps with chronic physical or emotional pain, or a chronic illness like multiple sclerosis or cancer, we explore what led up to the illness or pain issue. We often discover that these people take care of everyone else first and put themselves last. Consequently, they never get around to taking care of themselves. They don't take time to eat well, exercise, sleep enough or even relax. Are you one of those people? Taking care of everyone else and putting ourselves last takes a toll on us. It's a common issue for many people. At some level, maybe they don't think they are worthy. They have a belief that other people are worth more or that they have a duty to provide for others, but not themselves.

I suggest making a list of your priorities in life. What's important to you? The list probably includes things like family, spirituality, work, etc. Sometimes we are at the bottom or aren't even on the list. We really need to be at top in order to be the person we want to be for others. If we are not taking care of ourselves, we deplete our energy and are unable to provide the way we want to for others.

Where are you on your list?

Sometimes people think it's selfish to take care of themselves first or rank first on their list of priorities. I think people get the words selfish and self-care confused. The truth is simple: if we don't take care of ourselves first, we are in no position to care for others. So why do we go on and on, and give and give until we're emotionally and physically exhausted? When flight attendants give the safety instructions on the airplane before takeoff, they always tell you to put on your own oxygen mask before assisting others. There is a good reason for that! You can't help others unless you take care of yourself first.

Attitude of Gratitude

Feeling gratitude is a choice we make. Research shows that simply focusing each day on three to five things for which we can be grateful will increase our health and happiness. For an even stronger dose of health and happiness, express your gratitude to someone else. Holding the thought of gratitude and expressing it to a good friend will benefit you as well. People with an attitude of gratitude are healthier, sleep better, and tend to exercise more. Gratitude is a way of being in which you notice and appreciate the positives in the world. As such, gratitude is an important part of well-being.

Gratitude practiced daily will strengthen your immune system and help you approach life with greater optimism. Even when things are not going well in our lives, we can be grateful for something. Just being alive, for one, or having a job, enough money for lunch, or a place to live, are things to appreciate. I challenge everyone to commit to being thankful and appreciating life every day. Pausing in our busy lives and feeling gratitude promotes good health. Life is good!

My previously mentioned patient, "Tammy," had been in a job she loved for many years. Then the job changed. She had less responsibility, less freedom and more scrutiny. Tammy could easily see the situation as a demotion and feel "less than," critical of herself and her work environment. Instead, she chose to find the blessings in the job change and created a whole new job for herself. She focused on the things she could control and found happiness. Her boss, who had been putting her under the microscope, suddenly stopped criticizing her. Every time she criticized her, Tammy would just say "OK," smile, and find even more ways to create a job she loved. She accepted what it was, harvested the good from it, and let go of the rest. It turned out to be the best change in her career. She was close to retirement, and it wound up being a great way to end her career at this company. She saw it as a way to put more things on her resume, should she want to work somewhere else. She was happier than she had been at her job in years. She had more flexibility, freedom, and enjoyed herself each day. Before, she would have never taken time off, and now she felt OK taking care of herself. She was grateful for what she had and for her situation every day.

Several studies have indicated that daily gratitude results in higher reported levels of alertness, enthusiasm, determination, optimism and energy. Additionally, people experience less depression and stress, and are more likely to help others, exercise, and make progress toward personal goals. People with an "attitude of gratitude" have lower stress hormone levels, like cortisol.

Work gratitude into your day and improve your health!

Many of us face detours in life when things don't go as planned: struggling with an illness, a relationship, or a job; loss of a loved one; or an accident. We experience disappointment with an outcome or we have to take a timeout because of relationship issues, our work life or an illness. If you are struggling with a detour in your life, just believe that you will be back on the road again soon – and it may be an even better road than the previous one. I believe our thoughts influence our outcomes. Regardless of the difficulties we have or the detours on which we find ourselves, our thoughts can influence our situation. Detours are a part of life, and how long we stay on them depends on our thoughts and feelings. Just reach for a better-feeling thought.

We often don't have to go far to find someone in a worse situation than ours. Their situation puts things into perspective and may make our problems seem not so bad. Remember, things could always be worse, and we can be thankful for our current situation. There is always more than one way to look at something. We could say, "Oh, this is terrible," and that puts us down toward the bottom of that twelve-inch ruler. Or, we can look at it and say, "All right, I'm here, but I'm not there, so I'm grateful for that." For example, I am so blessed and grateful every day that my life only took a detour with our accident, and now I am back on the road again. I see many people who did not have the good outcome that I did.

There has been a lot of research done on the importance of gratitude, whether it's based on something you currently have or are just pretending to have. There are many ways you can begin to incorporate gratitude into your life. A great way to end each day is to think of a few things for which you are grateful. Make a list, or an inventory, of the day and notice things for which you're grateful.

You can continue to be grateful for similar things each day or try to find something different every day. The first ten to twenty days of this might not be difficult, but it gets harder as you have to think beyond the "easy" things to list. The benefit of doing this right before you go to bed is that you want those positive thoughts to be in your mind in those last moments as you drift off to sleep. Taking time to appreciate all the good things in your life is a good way to do it.

Even if you are struggling, you're grateful for something. You want to be thinking of things that make you feel good, and feeling gratitude leaves us with a good feeling. Remember, if you feel good, your vibration is higher. In order to increase your vibration, practice gratitude before you go to bed so that you end the day on a positive note.

Anger and Forgiveness

The relationship between forgiveness and health is significant. The fact is that after we have been hurt, humiliated or angered – whether it is real or imagined – not forgiving blocks the flow of love and adversely affects our energy. It profoundly affects our bodily functions, including our health. For example, our muscles may tighten, or we may get headaches, pain in our neck, arms and legs, or a sick feeling in our stomach. It affects the way we supply oxygen and nutrients to our cells. This increases the likelihood of inadequate repair during sleep. We need that sleep to recharge. Our teeth might clench if our jaw is tight, blood flow to our heart may constrict, and our digestion may be impaired. With our breathing restricted and our immune system depressed, we become vulnerable to infections, perhaps even cancers. When we feel badly, our mind is less able to see its way through problems and difficulties. The list goes on and on. Getting in touch with and releasing our bad feelings safely is important. So what about self-forgiveness? When we don't forgive, the effects can include feelings of depression, low self-acceptance, and a sense that we aren't worthy. We deprive ourselves of good life opportunities, punishing ourselves through activities or relationships that cause harm, addictions and so forth. Not being able to forgive ourselves or others negatively affects our energy and our lives. Our negative and critical thoughts about others and ourselves can have a tremendous impact. The word "negative" means to subtract from, and when we are negative, we subtract something from ourselves, and from the love and the life force that is potentially here for all of us to share. When we are stuck in a negative place, we delay healing for our body, emotions and relationships. In school, we do not learn how to forgive. We learn reading, writing and mathematics, but we do not learn the process of forgiveness. Yet it is important. To forgive others or ourselves, we have to begin with identifying where to utilize the forgiveness process. We first must become aware that, deep down, we value health, love and joy more than any disease, resentment or anger. We then must choose to forgive both ourselves and others from a place of love and compassion.

Let's take the example of being angry with someone because of something they did. If you follow one of the basic, core guidelines and accept that everyone does the best they can with what they have, we realize they did the best they could. That person may have been wrong, but perhaps they were not in a good place at the time. The same holds true for you. Be forgiving of yourself, too, because I'm sure you always do the best you can with what you have. People usually don't intentionally do things to make others angry. Remember, it is what it is. Accept it and harvest the good from it. You can always find something good. Forgiving someone does not mean that you agree with what they did, or that you condone or excuse their behavior. It simply means that you love them unconditionally. It separates the person from the event or incident.

An even harder task is forgiving ourselves, separating ourselves from the event or incident that took place. People often have an easier time forgiving other people than forgiving themselves. Oftentimes when we find ourselves becoming angry with other people, it's not so much what they have done, but a previous experience we have had that may be triggering our emotion. You actually are lowering your vibration. Remember, that means what you attract in the future will be a match to your current vibration, so you will get more of the same.

Anger and forgiveness are difficult things to deal with. If you have guilt, you are angry with yourself. It is really anger turned inward. Emotions like anger and hatred don't make us feel well. Many of us need to work on forgiveness on a regular basis. Self-acceptance means accepting yourself the way you are at any moment in time, knowing that you are perfect just the way you are. Self-acceptance is a difficult thing for people and often we get stuck.

I see people with chronic illnesses, and often they will say, "I just want my life back. I want to be normal. I miss being normal." They may become angry about not being normal anymore. Well, things happen in our lives. It doesn't matter what it is – getting married, changing a job, having an illness or an accident – really, just about anything. When you think about it, our lives are never really able to return to where they were originally. Throughout life, we end up having to continually create a new normal.

"MaryBeth" was talking about what "normal" is and related how the late humorist Erma Bombeck said normal was a setting on the washing machine. I thought that was a good definition of normal because, really, who knows what normal is?

Imagery Exercise: Forgiveness

"First, find a comfortable position and focus on your breathing. Inhale, breathing the fresh air in through your nose, into your lungs and down into your abdomen. Relax your abdomen, allowing it to deflate, letting all tension and discomfort float away with the exhalation. (Take a few breaths.) Now, take a slow, deep breath and let it out slowly. Take another even deeper breath and slowly exhale, allowing all remaining tension to float away with the breath. I am going to take you to a special place where you will feel very safe.

"You are in a forest, with lush green ferns and moss along the path. There are scattered light beams coming down through the trees. The path is soft and you are feeling so relaxed as you walk along, noticing all the smells and sounds of the forest. Butterflies flit about, greeting you. You may hear birds singing, and notice a small bunny as it eats grass at the side of the path. The path leads to a clearing in the forest, although it is not very sunny. A wooden fence surrounds the clearing, and people are in this fenced-in area. You can't really see them yet, as you are still too far away.

"As you walk closer, curious, you may recognize these people. You approach the gate and open it. You feel compelled to come into this area, and you feel very safe and relaxed. These are people who need your forgiveness. Whom do you recognize? Notice each person. Perhaps you even see yourself. You slowly make your way up to someone, and bless him or her with a loving intention and forgive them. You may want to give them a hug or embrace. They are so grateful for your forgiveness.

"Now you go up to each person, one at a time, and bless them with a loving intention, compassion, and forgiveness. (Pause) As you forgive them, they are grateful to you and are allowed to leave the clearing. As you bless and forgive each person, you bring peace to yourself, and it feels so good. You are feeling more relaxed and warm inside. You are finding a peace that has eluded you in the past.

"You notice, as people are leaving, the clearing is becoming brighter and the sun is beginning to shine. Soon there is only one person left. You bless them with a loving intention and forgive them. Everyone is gone; they have all left the forest. You are alone in the clearing. You look up at the beautiful sky and feel the sun warming your whole body. Your heart is light, and you are at peace. You look up at the sky and, perhaps, smile up at God or you look up to the sun, and feel thankful for finally being free. You give thanks for all those who have forgiven you as well, and you, too, leave the clearing.

"On your return journey down the path, your step is light and you notice even more beauty in the forest than you did before. The greens are greener, the sun shines brighter, and the smells more fragrant. Soon you are to the edge of the forest. You feel unburdened and carefree. You take a long, deep breath in and let it out slowly. Take another, even deeper breath and exhale slowly. You now begin to feel the surface beneath you (chair, bed table, etc.). You may hear sounds in the room.

"When you are ready, slowly open your eyes to a soft gaze and stretch if you feel like it, as you become aware of your surroundings."

Imagery Exercise: The Setting Sun

You can use this imagery exercise to control and reduce emotional or physical discomfort, providing well-being, comfort, and ease.

"To begin, get in a comfortable position and focus on your breathing. Feel the breath come in through your nose, to your sinuses, and down all the way to your abdomen. It fills your abdomen with relaxation. As you exhale, your abdomen deflates and all tensions flow away with the breath. With each comfortable breath, tension flows out of your body. Take a slow, deep breath, and let it out slowly and fully. Take another even deeper breath, and let it out slowly and fully.

"Now I'd like you to imagine a special sunset, one that has the power to ease pain and discomfort. Imagine you are lying or sitting on a beautiful beach, the sand is still warm from the day's sun. The sand is soft and fine, as it supports every part and curve of your body, providing a wonderful cushion beneath you. Notice what you see in your surroundings. Notice what you hear, perhaps the gentle waves on the beach. Can you smell the clean air of the ocean breeze? Take in the clean, fresh air, and bring it into your lungs and abdomen to relax every part or your body.

"Notice what the temperature is like, as you rest comfortably on the beach at sunset. Notice all the images around you, the colors, perhaps there is wildlife, perhaps there are other people there, or perhaps you are there by yourself. Your eyes now focus on the beautiful sunset before you. Imagine whatever colors you see. The skies are brilliant, and you have never seen such beauty. The patterns of colorful clouds speak peacefully to you. The sun is just about to set on the horizon line of the water. The bottom of the bright sun is just barely touching the horizon.

"You watch as the sun slowly begins to set, first covering only a small portion of it. You may realize, as the sun is getting smaller, as it sets into the horizon, that your discomfort is lessening. You may even notice that with each breath you take, as you exhale, the sun lets a little more of your discomfort diminish. Soon you realize that you can push the sun down into the water with each breath, and you can lessen your discomfort… a little more of your discomfort leaves you each time you exhale. As the sun gets smaller and smaller, your discomfort becomes less and less.

"As you breathe, the sun continues to set, and now you are confident you can control the sunset and your discomfort. You had the power all the time, and this magic sunset is your vehicle to take control of the pain. With each breath, you feel stronger and stronger, confident you can eliminate the pain from your body. The sun is setting on your terms now, and your pain is under your control. Continue breathing slowly and deeply until all discomfort has left your body, mind, and spirit. (Pause)

"The sun has set and there is a warm blanket of deep-blue, peaceful tranquility around you. Enjoy this time and peacefulness. Breathe in the fresh, clean ocean fragrance; feel the comfort your body feels without pain and *discomfort. (Pause) You know now that you can visit this sunset at any time and control your pain, whatever it may be.*

"Once again, you sense the soft, warm sand beneath your body, supporting it. Now you begin to sense the (table, chair, or bed) below you, supporting you. You may be aware of sounds in the room. You begin to be aware of your position, wriggling your fingers and toes. When you are ready, you may open your eyes to a soft gaze."

Imagery Exercise: To Alleviate Physical Pain

"To begin, get in a comfortable position, close your eyes, and focus all your attention on your breathing. Breathe in through your nose. Feel the air coming in through your nose, and going down to your abdomen; as you slowly exhale, let your abdomen relax and deflate. Feel the tension flowing from your body with each exhalation. You may want to take a signal breath, letting your body know it's time to go inside and relax. Exhale your breath completely, then take a big breath in through your nose and let it all out through your mouth.

"Continue to breathe this way, breathing comfortably. ... Take a few more breaths and then take a deep, full breath and exhale slowly and deeply. Take another full, even deeper breath and exhale slowly. You may notice that you are somewhat more relaxed than when you started.

"Now I want you to imagine a table before you and on that table is a bucket. Notice what the table looks like. What color is it? Is it wooden or something else? Reach out and touch it if you like. Notice the bucket on the table and look inside. In the bucket is a cool, glistening liquid. This liquid is able to anesthetize anything it touches. Notice what the liquid looks like. ... You can dip your finger in it, if you'd like, and feel the coolness, the numbness in your finger. Swirl your finger around the cool, soft, glistening liquid. Now you can dip your other fingers in and swirl slowly, putting your hand in deeper and deeper in the cool, anesthetizing liquid; deeper and deeper, your hand is feeling colder and more numb with every swirl in the bucket.

"Continue doing this until your hand is completely numb, feeling heavy, like a piece of wood. Once your hand is completely numb, taking as long as you need, you realize you can transfer this numbness to any part of your body, any part of your body that hurts. Your hand with the cool, magic liquid will numb that area, too.

"Put your hand on anything that hurts and feel the cool, numbing feeling transfer to that area ... so that it feels cold and heavy, numb. Transfer all the pain from that area to your hand now. Knowing that you can dip your hand *back in the anesthetizing liquid in the bucket to numb the hand again ... taking the pain away from your hand, leaving it in the bucket where it will be transformed into the cool, glistening liquid. . You can go back and forth from the bucket of anesthetizing liquid to your area of pain as many times as you need to in order to numb the area and provide relief.*

"Know you can do this as much and as often as you need to, whenever you want, by simply relaxing and imagining the bucket of anesthetizing, cool, glistening liquid before you and dipping your hand, swirling it around until your hand feels cold, numb, like a piece of wood, and placing it on the area of pain. Do this as often and as much as you need to for comfort and to provide relief."

Summary and Suggestions

How do you see the world? We see and experience what we think about. We should put ourselves near the top of our priorities. When we are, we take better care of ourselves. Good nutrition and moving our body helps our brain think better, improves our mood, and adds to our well-being. Gratitude practiced daily will strengthen our immune system. When we are not able to forgive, we are the only one who suffers.

- Notice all of the "so-what" issues in your life.
- Choose to take care of your body by eating well.
- Eat fresh foods and shop around the outside of the grocery store.
- Balance your blood sugar by eating a combination of proteins, carbohydrates and fats.
- Breathe and relax to lower your stress hormones, like cortisol.
- Water your brain. Drink at least eight glasses of water a day.
- If you think you might have food sensitivities, try an elimination diet.
- Practice good sleep habits.
- Notice where you are on your list of priorities.

Many of us spend our days being busy and thinking about what we have to do, and never really living our lives. Dwelling in the past can lead to depression; worrying about the future generates anxiety. In the next section we will discuss the importance of experiencing the present.

Fourth Key – Experience Every Moment As It Is

"Mindfulness means paying attention in a particular way: on purpose, in the present moment, and nonjudgmentally."
- Jon Kabat-Zinn

In the West, the field of psychology developed a therapeutic practice starting in the 1970s called mindfulness. It has its roots in the Buddhist meditation practice of awareness. Jon Kabat-Zinn is a teacher of mindfulness meditation and the founder of the Mindfulness-Based Stress Reduction program at the University of Massachusetts Medical Center in Worcester, Mass. In his book, *Wherever You Go There You Are,* he talks about how mindfulness is really paying attention on purpose.

Mindfulness involves a conscious direction of our awareness. It refers to a psychological quality that involves bringing one's complete attention to the present on a moment-to-moment basis. It involves experiencing the present and noticing "what is" in a nonjudgmental way. It requires us to keep our minds absorbed right here in this moment, noticing the details and nuances of our actions. For example, if we eat an apple with mindfulness, we notice the texture, the aroma, the feeling of taking a bite, the crunching sound we hear, and how the juice squirts out as we bite into it. We notice everything there is to notice about eating and really tasting that apple.

The most basic form of mindfulness practice is observing the breath. To observe means not to participate, but just to notice. Rather than entering into thoughts, emotions and sensations, we simply observe and let them pass away without being drawn into them. In Western culture, our hectic lifestyle, many responsibilities, and chaos of life can make the pursuit of mindfulness seem almost unattainable. Work, family, finances and a multitude of other pressures vying for our attention distract our mind. It is little wonder that most of us usually feel stressed, overwhelmed and on the cusp of burnout.

Mindfulness refers to being completely in touch with and aware of the present moment, as well as taking a nonjudgmental approach to our inner experience. For example, a mindful approach to one's inner experience is simply viewing "thoughts as thoughts" as opposed to evaluating thoughts as positive or negative. Mindfulness simply refers to observing and noticing without judgment. It is what it is. It's noticing the mind's tendency to be pulled in new directions, and simply bringing our attention back to the present moment.

Mindfulness is widely recognized as a healthy way to manage stress and improve well-being. It is practiced in many different ways. Mindfulness practice brings focus to selected objects, such as the sensation of breathing, with awareness to the present moment with nonjudgmental acknowledgment of what is happening.

If we are thinking about the past or what we have to do, we never really get to enjoy right now. I often hear people say that life goes so fast, the kids grow up too quickly, and before you know it another month has passed. In our busy, complicated lives, we perhaps spend too much time pondering the trivial, dwelling on the past, or anticipating future possibilities. We tend to miss a full appreciation of the present; we miss out on the here and now. The time seems to go even faster. Kids do grow up quickly, but I believe that if we were more mindful of each moment, we would feel as though we are really living our lives. If we spend more time thinking about what happened or what's going to happen, do we really ever spend any time living?

By experiencing a situation mindfully through your senses, we allow ourselves to respond naturally rather than react mindlessly. Mindfulness allows us to see things more clearly in any situation so we can respond effectively rather than have a knee-jerk reaction. By practicing mindfulness on a regular basis, we can learn to see how our thoughts, images, emotions and physical body interact. Mindfulness can greatly enhance emotional stability by keeping us in touch with the part of us that knows how to self-regulate and not just fly off the handle. If your life seems like a continuous drama, you probably are disconnected and feel stressed out most of the time.

A practice of mindfulness can help you get to that observing role, allowing you to see things as they are, without the drama. To be mindful, we must choose to be an observer of our own life as it unfolds in the present without judging what we see as good or bad. Mindfulness is paying attention intentionally with a nonjudgmental attitude of acceptance, openness, curiosity, kindness, patience and surrender. It is the raw awareness of what is happening now without judgment, commentary or decision. It is observing and experiencing without reacting. Mindfulness brings the mind and body together in the same place at the same time.

Mindful Meditation

A great way to develop the practice of being mindful is to meditate. Many people think the only way to meditate is to sit cross-legged, empty your mind, and be still for a long period of time. Although you can meditate that way, there really are many ways to live in the present moment and practice meditation in your daily life. Meditation does not necessarily mean clearing your mind of all thought and having an empty mind. When practiced, however, it slows thought and allows you to clear your mind. It is directed concentration, focusing your attention on something so intently that the mind chatter falls away and you feel calm and peaceful.

Meditation usually is directed toward an object. Often people use their breath as a focus of their attention. We have to breathe anyway; the breath is always with us – no special equipment is needed. The breath is a good place to start, but the focus can be any number of things, such as a candle flame, mantra (a repeated word or phrase), sound, image or prayer. Saying the Rosary is a form of meditation, as it's a repetitive prayer. You also can incorporate imagery as a guided meditation. You can practice mindfulness when gazing at a beautiful sunset, taking in the beauty of that one moment without thinking about the future or the past, focusing so intently on that present moment that your thoughts stop wandering and your mind is still.

Our subconscious mind generally has all the answers we need, but often we are not quiet or still enough to hear them. Meditation helps you hear the answers. I challenge you to be still and listen to your inner voice. If there is a question you have, just ask. If you are still enough, you will hear the answer.

Living in the Present

When you practice living in the present moment on a daily basis, your life can be the same or even more stressful, but it won't bother you as much. Feelings of distress usually aren't directly related to an event or situation that occurs, but rather our reaction to it and the thoughts we have about it. Meditation helps you minimize your reactions by keeping you focused on the present moment.

There are many benefits of mindfulness and meditation. They help increase the activity of the parasympathetic nervous system, our involuntary nervous system. The parasympathetic nervous system is like our autopilot. It's the relaxing part of us. It keeps us sitting up straight; it keeps us breathing; it keeps our heart beating. It's always working. Its counterpart is the sympathetic nervous system, which is the flight or fright response. An over-active sympathetic nervous system is the cause of many of today's health problems.

Our bodies are not meant to withstand the everyday, chronic type of stress that we have in our lives today. Originally, humans had to deal with the occasional life-threatening stress of being attacked by an animal, such as a saber-tooth tiger. Today, it's as though the tiger never goes away. It is always there, and consequently, we are never fully relaxed. The increase in stress hormones like cortisol can lead to high blood pressure, heart palpitations, anxiety, headaches, decreased immune function, skin and gastrointestinal problems, and weight gain.

Creating balance through breath control, guided relaxation, meditation and visualization will slow the heart rate, lower blood pressure and cholesterol levels, reduce anxiety, increase creativity, and strengthen the immune system. It's useful for any issue that is stress driven – and most physical and emotional health issues we face in today's world are stress driven. Sometimes I think our entire society has ADD (attention deficit disorder). If you concentrate on your mind for thirty seconds, notice how many times you interrupt yourself.

The present moment is really the only moment that we have. Mindful meditation focuses on something like your breath and being present for that moment – just being aware of what is. We need to take time out of our day and reclaim this moment, making nothing happen, making no judgments, by being still and giving ourselves back the wonderful gift of now.

Today's world is fast-paced and busy. We don't take the time to just be. Remember that saying about becoming human "doings" instead of human beings? I think this is true. Creating balance in this way increases the release of the "feel good" chemicals in your brain, like beta endorphins, which help us feel calm and relaxed. Meditation is one way to release the brain chemicals that make us feel good and promote better health.

Mindfulness Meditation Practice

Here are some tips for beginning a formal meditation practice. You can use anything for the subject of focus, of course, but the breath is certainly an easy place to start. I would suggest meditating at the same time every day. Many people find that first thing in the morning is a nice time to meditate; other people find the end of the day works better; or, maybe you need to take a break in the middle of the workday.

If you set a time, you are more likely to begin developing the habit of practicing routinely. For me, I find that if I don't meditate in the morning, the day gets away from me and I don't get to it. So find a time that works for you and stick to it. Set an appointment with yourself every day; write it in your calendar. You are worth making an appointment with yourself!

Be as free as possible from distractions. Choose a quiet and comfortable place to meditate where nobody is going to bother you. You may want to make that place special – light a candle or burn some incense. Sit in a chair, maybe it's a special chair, or on the floor with your head, neck and back straight but not stiff. In my world, I have a chair that I sit in every day to meditate. If you are in the same position in the chair, if you are in the same room, if things are the same, it becomes a habit and soon you will be able to quickly drop down to that metaphorical point thirty to fifty feet below the surface of the water. It will be familiar to you, and your mind will associate sitting that way with relaxing and meditating.

Bring awareness in the first few moments that you are awake; it's a good time for people who say they don't have time to meditate. I often ask people if they have a snooze button on their alarm clock and most say yes. Depending on the alarm clock you have, it gives you seven to nine minutes of meditation time if you just hit the snooze but don't go back to sleep. Choose to just be aware of everything, conscious of everything, and in that present moment until you get out of bed. Often the alarm goes off and either we hit the snooze and go back to sleep, or we just jump out of bed. Either way, we are missing the present moment.

When you meditate, particularly for the first time, don't expect some altered state of consciousness or big epiphany. It's called a practice for a reason. For some people, the big epiphany doesn't happen for a very long time; for others, it occurs more quickly. If you feel disappointed, you may not continue with the practice. Weave meditation into the fabric of your life; don't just do it when stressed. Develop mindfulness as a way of being rather than just a technique. After some practice, it will come naturally.

You can incorporate mindfulness into your everyday life in many things that you already do. Mindful eating is a good way to start, and it can make the difference between eating a whole bag of chips or just two or three chips. When we are unaware of what we are eating, we may eat too fast or become distracted. When we are thinking about something else, we miss the whole experience and pleasure of eating. Being mindful and noticing nuances of the experience slows us down, and more importantly, allows us to experience, enjoy and savor our food.

Sometimes when we eat too fast, our brain doesn't get the signal that we are full. It takes about twenty minutes for the brain to get that message. This leads to overeating. Stop this by taking three slow deep breaths and remind yourself to enjoy a moment of mindfulness. Smile and express gratitude for the nourishing food you have. Take a moment to notice the color and appearance of the food. Give gratitude to the cook, even if it's you.

For your first bite, take a really long time to chew your food. Chew it many times, fifteen to twenty times if you can. Notice how it feels in your mouth, the textures and the tastes. Savor the flavor, the color, the aroma and the texture. Be grateful for this moment and open up to it.

Mindful Eating Practice

Jon Kabat-Zinn introduced the following Buddhist technique at a stress-reduction clinic many years ago. I often use it as an illustration.

You will need a raisin and a clock or timer. The goal is to spend three to five minutes eating one raisin. It's all about noticing and being present. Most people laugh when I tell them we are going to spend all that time eating one raisin, because they have never tried it. How often do we eat and not really experience the food? Learning this technique can show you how to feel more satisfied eating just a couple M&Ms versus a whole bag.

First, pick up the raisin and look at it. Notice wrinkles, the color, the fragrance, how it feels between your fingers. When you have noticed everything there is to notice about this raisin, put it up to your lips (not in your mouth yet). Just touch it to your lips and see what you notice. How does it feel? Notice the texture, the wrinkles, the firmness, and again, how it smells. Next, put the raisin in your mouth, but don't bite it right away, just roll it around on your tongue and see what you notice. We have different taste buds on different parts of our tongue, so in different places in your mouth, it may have a different taste. Again, notice the texture and the wrinkles. You may be able to detect an aroma, as there is an open connection between our mouth and our nose (the pharynx). Just keep rolling the raisin around, noticing everything possible. It may change in texture and become softer or spongier.

Watch the clock or timer and see how much time has passed. Remember the goal is to take three to five minutes to eat this raisin. When you have noticed all you can about the raisin, and how it has changed since you started this exercise, you can bite into it. Don't chew it all at once; just take a bite and let it squish between your teeth. Notice what it feels like, the flavor, the sweetness, the texture, the aroma. Continue to chew it slowly and enjoy its entire flavor.

The response I often get from people who try this exercise is that they never realized or noticed how much flavor is in just one raisin. This exercise allows you to savor the eating experience. That's what can make the difference between just a little bit of something or the whole bag. In other words, when we don't pay attention to what we are doing, we are not mindful and present. We don't get the full experience.

As a result of this exercise, my experience eating a candy bar has changed. One bite now feels like an entire candy bar, and I feel satisfied as I truly savor it. If I am mindful and eat it slowly, paying attention to the act of eating it, that one bite of dark chocolate (my favorite) is more gratifying than a larger amount. It makes eating chocolate a good thing as I don't feel like I overindulged. Sometimes when I am not paying attention, or multitasking and forgetting to be present, I'll automatically eat the whole piece of chocolate without realizing it. I look around and it's gone. I don't even remember I ate it, and I didn't really taste and enjoy it. Being mindful during eating can make a difference in how much we eat.

Incorporate Mindfulness into Your Life

We also can be mindful while driving. The unconscious mind takes over the wheel after we learn to drive and it will pull the conscious mind in if necessary. If we are actually being mindful, we will be more attentive while driving. We notice how we feel in the vehicle, our state of alertness and the surroundings. We notice our breathing, the sensation of our hands on the steering wheel, all the information that is coming through our eyes and ears. Accidents often happen when we are not paying attention.

We also can be mindful while walking or running. When I first started my meditation practice years ago, I had a difficult time sitting still, so I began meditating while jogging. I would pace my breathing to my stride and focus on that. Eventually, I was able to sit and meditate.

You also can do it by pacing your breathing to your stride whether you are walking or jogging. If you do mindfulness meditative walking, you actually walk slowly, being mindful of every movement. As you walk, breathe in and slowly raise your foot, then slowly lower your foot to the ground as you breathe out.

You can practice mindfulness in front of the mirror, too. How often do you look at yourself in the mirror when you brush your teeth? Stand in front of the mirror and take some breaths in and out. Relax for a moment, look into the mirror with new eyes, and notice yourself in the mirror. Look into your eyes. Now brush your teeth mindfully – slowly, carefully, paying attention to how you are doing it, how it feels. Notice the taste and how fresh your mouth feels. Express gratitude for your teeth, for having a healthy mouth, gums and tongue, and for the role they play in your body.

You can practice mindfulness while waiting for an appointment. How many times have you arrived early at the doctor's office, as an example, or you've just had to wait somewhere? How often do you stand in line at the grocery store or at the department store? Rather than feeling stressed, why not take those extra minutes to practice mindfulness? That takes the judgment out of the equation as well. If you just take some breaths, attend to and explore the moment, be conscious, awake, aware, and notice your surroundings, it will be a different experience. I would bet the line will seem to go faster. These are just a few ways you can incorporate mindfulness into your daily activities.

Practice in Meditation

"Find a posture that feels comfortable to you and establish yourself in your body, lying, sitting, etc. If you choose a straight-back chair, sit erect and not leaning on the back of the chair or on a cushion. Do something comfortable with your hands. It's easiest in the beginning to just close your eyes because it blocks out the sensory distractions, especially when you're just starting. You

also can keep them halfway open, but focused downward. The goal is to stay attentive and not fall asleep; the intention is to 'fall awake.'

"Breathe through your nose as best you can. It activates the parasympathetic nervous system. Begin experiencing the flowing of your own breath ... just experiencing the feeling of the breath entering the body and leaving the body ... moment by moment and breath by breath.

"You can follow the breath in any number of places; feel the air moving in through the nostrils, or feeling the belly rise and fall. Dwell here, riding on the motion of your breath, allowing the experience of the full sensation of the in-breath, the pause and the full sensation of the out-breath ... and the pause as the breath bottoms out before the next breath.

"Experience the breath without trying to change it, push it or pull it, no judgment, just experience, in and out of the body. (Pause) Riding on the motion of the breath, as though you are on a horse on the merry-go-round, going up and down, up and down, with the breath ... on the motion of your own breath, moment by moment. (Pause)

"Whether you're just beginning to practice meditation or you have been doing this for a long time, you may find your mind will wander off somewhere. Just because you are riding the motion of your breath doesn't mean your mind will stay there; it will go off someplace else -- maybe to the future, starting to plan or worry, or to the past, or just judging your experience, wondering, 'Am I doing this right?' Just note this means you are in your thoughts. When you notice, take a moment to acknowledge your thought and then reconnect with the breath.

"In the process, gently escorting the mind back to the breath, don't scold or judge. The mind will just wander; it's natural. When you notice this, just notice the thought and gently bring your attention back to the breath. The breath is the focus; nothing else matters right now. . . . If your mind wanders fifty times, just notice, let go and re-establish the connection with the breath. Allow yourself to comfortably sit in silence; just being here attending to the breath. It is a gift to yourself. Just this moment ... just this breath coming in, just this breath going out. Practice as though it's the only thing there is to do. This is a powerful practice that you can keep up for long periods of time.

"You can expand the field of awareness -- include the breath, but also include your body as a whole, your awareness of your inhabiting the body, breathing. Feel your skin breathing, feel the movements of the breath, wherever they predominate, simply be aware of the breath as a whole, in the body, in silence, fully awake.

"The longer we sit this way, the more you may become aware of stiffness in the body because we are not moving. Various sensations may grow in intensity and may grow to discomfort, maybe even to pain, but you can be work with this. Just hold it, be loving and gentle to the sensation without trying to make the discomfort or pain go away or change. The breath can move into those areas where the discomfort or intensity is, and the breath itself may have an effect on the discomfort or pain. We can even hold unpleasant sensations in awareness, with greater connection to our body."

Some tips for beginning a formal meditation practice (substitute any object of focus for the breath):

- Meditate at the same time every day; early morning works well for many people.
- Be as free as possible from distractions. Choose a place to meditate where nothing and no one will bother you.
- Bring awareness in the first few moments you are awake; don't just jump out of bed as though you're on autopilot. You also can bring awareness at the end of the day.
- Wear comfortable, nonrestrictive clothing.
- Meditation is the work of a lifetime, that's why they call it a practice. Begin with what you think you can do and start with just a few minutes. Work your way up.
- Don't expect to have an altered state of consciousness or some wonderful experience right away. You need to stick with it over time. If you expect something else, you'll be disappointed.
- When ending your meditation session, if your eyes are closed, allow them to slowly open.
- Taking a deep breath or stretching is sometimes helpful.
- Weave meditation into the fabric of your life. Don't use it just when you're stressed; it's a way of being rather than a technique. After some practice, it will come naturally when you are stressed.
- Incorporate meditation into your daily life. Simply take a moment to connect with your breath while doing routine tasks, such as arriving early for an appointment, standing in the checkout line, eating, or even washing the dishes.
- Take moments in your day to pay attention to your breath and be mindful of the present moment without thinking about the future or the past. Just enjoy the now.

Summary and Suggestions

Mindfulness is being aware and paying attention to the present moment, noticing, without judgment. The focus of mindfulness meditation is not to necessarily clear your mind of all thoughts; rather it is to focus on something so intently that the rest of the mind chatter falls away. Mindfulness meditation slows the heart rate, lowers blood pressure and cholesterol levels, reduces anxiety, increases creativity, and strengthens the immune system.

- Practice being present in your life and paying attention, without judgment; just notice.
- Begin a mindfulness meditation practice. Start with what you can do, be gentle and non-judgmental.
- If you have many thoughts, just acknowledge them and then return to whatever you've chosen to focus on.
- Your breath is a simple and always available focus of attention.
- Try eating mindfully, and allow yourself to really taste and savor your food.
- Incorporate mindfulness into your daily life – while you are waiting in line at the store, washing dishes or taking a walk, for example.

Unconditional love, of others and ourselves, is the foundation of achieving a life of joy. Next we will explore how spirituality intertwines with unconditional love to help us find the joy we all deserve.

Fifth Key – It's All About Love

"Love yourself, love your neighbor, love your enemies, but begin with self-love. You cannot love others until you love yourself. You cannot share what you do not have. If you do not love yourself, you cannot love anyone else either."
~ don Miguel Ruiz, author and founder of the Sixth Sun Foundaton

The most fundamental characteristic of God and spirituality is that it offers us the experience of unconditional love. That is, no matter how another person acts or appears, we have compassion and care for them without judgment. Conditional love disappears when certain conditions are no longer fulfilled. Unconditional love shows up both in our increased capacity to give love to others and to experience more love coming into our lives. Sometimes our biggest challenge is loving ourselves unconditionally. This kind of love manifests itself through the experience of having everything we need in our life and being happy. Many people think they love themselves, but it is usually based on conditions. If you get upset with yourself because you made a mistake or you don't think you are thin enough, smart enough, good enough, etc., you love yourself conditionally. If you love yourself unconditionally, those things don't matter.

Unconditional love means we recognize the divine within us, as well as within all people. Peace of mind and unconditional love for ourselves are important for living an abundant life.

Having feelings of love toward others and ourselves is critical when we fall asleep each night. Have you ever heard the saying, "Don't go to bed mad?" That is actually good advice. The conscious mind takes a break as you sleep; our subconscious mind stays very active. Because of this, the thoughts we think about before we drift off to sleep are vitally important. Feeling love and appreciation, and having positive thoughts in those moments just before falling asleep is healthy for us. Knowing that you are good, loveable, and worthy of respect is the key.

The more you love yourself, the easier it becomes for you to spend time with yourself and actually enjoy the silence of your own thoughts, ideas and personality. It also tells the universe that you deserve those things you desire and want in your life, and allows the universe to begin to align itself in ways that will allow you to get what you want. If you love yourself, you know that you are worthy and you don't need to prove it to anyone. To love unconditionally means it doesn't matter what is going on in the outside world; it doesn't matter what the situation is, we just love regardless.

If you want to find out how you feel at a subconscious level about someone or yourself, simply use the muscle-testing technique described earlier. Say something positive about that person and follow it up with, "I forgive them and accept them as they are," or "I love them completely and unconditionally." We can use the same statements about ourselves. See if you get a positive response (muscle is strong) or negative response (there is weakness) when doing the muscle testing. If you hold on to anger and are not able to forgive, you are really depleting your body's energy.

Self-love is a condition of awareness and a way of perceiving. The art of loving yourself begins with self-acceptance. Self-acceptance is loving yourself unconditionally and being happy with who you are now. It's believing you are perfect just the way you are. This is not to say you don't want to change or improve, it simply means you love and accept yourself anyway. It's an agreement with yourself to appreciate, validate, accept and support who you are at this very moment. It is important to accept even those parts you want to change.

Our Heart - Another Brain?

When we think of love, we often think of a heart with a cupid or a Valentine's Day card. We also can consider our physical heart to be another brain. In addition to the brain in our head, we also have a "heart brain." The heart not only puts out its own hormones, but also instantaneously communicates electromagnetic and chemical information to the rest of the body and to other bodies near it. Our heart chakra, located in the center of our chest, is one of the main chakras where we take in all the love and healing energy the universe has to offer. We know feelings and information sent from the heart to the brain can have a profound effect on the how our brain functions and how we feel. The synchronization between the heart and the brain eliminates stress and permits a feeling of well-being. The heart is often called the home of the soul. When a person consciously focuses their attention on the heart, it affects the brain and the brain generally affects the body.

The energy of the heart can reach up to eight to ten feet beyond us. One person's heart signal can affect another's brainwaves, and heart-brain synchronization can occur between two people when they interact.

The Institute of HeartMath is an internationally recognized, nonprofit research and education organization dedicated to helping people reduce stress, self-regulate emotions, and build energy and resilience for healthy, happy lives. Find more information on HeartMath at www.heartmath.org.

Exercise: Taking in the Love

To do this exercise, first get into a comfortable position. Place your hands over your heart or on the center of your chest. We have energy centers, smaller *chakras,* in the palms of our hands, and this connects with the energy of our heart. Many people will notice they begin to feel warmth and experience a good feeling simply by doing this. It just feels good to place your hands there. As you breathe in through your nose, activating the relaxing side of you, imagine taking in all the love that's there for you. Perhaps it's love from your children, or your partner, a dear friend, your parents, or anything that helps you feel that warm, secure, loved feeling. For some people it may be a memory of the feeling they had when they just met their partner, that new-love feeling, the kind that makes you want to just be close to that person and enjoy every moment. Perhaps it's when you first held your new baby and felt that connection. It could even be your pet. Dogs are great at demonstrating unconditional love. You may have scolded your dog, and they love you just the same, it's unconditional.

As you breathe in all that love, notice how you feel, the warmth and joyful feeling you have. It's good to imagine unconditional self-love as well. This is good to practice, as we don't do this enough. This exercise is also a great way to fall asleep. It may even help you fall asleep faster. Put a hand on your heart if you are having a conversation that is upsetting to you. If you are on the phone, it's easy to hold the phone with one hand and place the other hand on your chest.

As you have your hands on your chest, you can send love to others as well. Imagine a pink color radiating from your heart and getting bigger and bigger as you continue to breathe. Then imagine a pink ribbon or stream of a pink color going out to the person to whom you want to send love. Imagine the pink color surrounding them and then penetrating them as it reaches their heart. Visualize this pink good feeling spreading throughout their body, until it fills their whole being. Imagine that they feel the same warmth that you do.

Spirituality – We Are Not Alone

Don't overlook spiritual health as an aspect of healing and well-being. It is beneficial to be consciously aware of the role the spirit plays in our lives. Being spiritually healthy also means being intimately connected to our surroundings, spouse, partner, family, friends and community. Spirituality is based on the belief that we are not alone in the universe. A variety of approaches, including prayer, meditation, gratitude and spending time within nature, can further deepen our awareness of ourselves as a spiritual, socially connected being.

Research shows that positive beliefs, comfort and strength gained from religion, meditation, prayer or believing in angels can contribute to a person's well-being. Improving your spiritual health may not cure an illness, but it may help you feel better and enjoy your life to the best of your ability. It also may help prevent some health problems.

Spirituality is the way we find meaning, hope, comfort and inner peace in our lives, knowing that we are loved, safe and protected. Many people define spirituality through religion. Others find it through music, art, a connection with nature, or just an inner knowing. Many times, we just use the term God, whether it's referring to the universe, source energy, cosmic consciousness, or just something we believe connects us. It is the sense that there is something greater, a web that connects all of us.

Spirituality can be different things to different people, and there is no single right or wrong way. We do know, however, that the mind, body and spirit are all connected.

To improve your spiritual health, contemplate and identify the things in your life that give you a sense of peace, inner comfort, support, strength and connection. Set aside time every day to do things that help cultivate your spirituality. This may include taking a walk in nature, volunteering, praying or meditating, singing, or just moving your body. Reading inspirational books or taking quiet time to just be can enhance a sense of well-being. Using a movement therapy like yoga or Qi-gong, playing a sport, attending religious services or Bible study also can help cultivate your spiritual health. We can feed our spirit in many ways.

When families and individuals face tough situations, including health problems, their religious and spiritual beliefs and practices may help fight feelings of helplessness, and aid in restoring meaning and order to the situation.

The main difference between spirituality and organized religion is the freedom to choose your own path toward enlightenment, and ultimately, recognition of the divine within ourselves. We are never alone. Our God, creator, universal intelligence, higher self, or whatever we choose to call it, is always with us and loves us unconditionally. We have a connection with an invisible network of assistance. By asking for help, we receive guidance and support. Doors that appeared closed miraculously open for us. It requires faith, patience, and letting go of expectations or preconceived ideas of the outcome or timing. Detaching from the outcome is sometimes difficult, but it may allow those doors to open. If we are struggling in some way, things just don't work. When we give up the struggle, detach from the outcome and come from a loving place, everything works better.

Have you ever experienced perfect timing – a moment when everything just seems to fall into place? Events come together with such exactness that it feels as though we are launched onto a pre-ordained course? We can't stop thinking about someone and we run into him or her on the street; a person we have just met offers us the perfect job; we miss our plane, and on the next flight, we sit next to someone with whom we fall in love. This is synchronicity, a state of grace.

"Melissa" and "Kyle" were struggling financially. Changes at their jobs left them financially strapped. As with so many people, Kyle found himself unemployed. They had planned a vacation more than a year earlier and had been looking forward to it for a long time. It was going to be the honeymoon they never had. Now, they didn't know how they were going to have enough money to enjoy themselves on their dream vacation. They had paid for the flights a year ago, but they now had no money to spend once they got there. They were just about to cancel their flight and stay home when they received a totally unexpected tax refund. They had not received a refund in more than ten years. It was the miracle they needed. They went on their vacation, the honeymoon they had waited for so long. A door opened when they didn't expect it.

Whatever your belief system is, it should be a source of love and support for you. Stress, trauma and crisis often interfere with our connection to our internal sense of knowing. We live in a culture that values the ability to achieve more in less time, and believes that the way to do this is to do more things at once. The end result is an inability to be fully aware of what's going on in and around you, a decrease of awareness and insight. Maybe we lose connection during a time of difficulty or pain, and this leaves us unable to make a big decision from a place of inner self-awareness and knowledge. Quiet time, self-reflection and meditation are wonderful ways to access that inner healer inside each of us.

Developing our relationship with the divine intelligence (God), loving ourselves and feeling appreciation for our lives are cornerstones to well-being. Asking questions and taking time to be quiet enough to hear the answers is something we all need to make time to do, or we won't see the signs and hear the answers. This doesn't have to take a lot of time. We all have mental moments in our day, time to pause and listen. We probably use that time now to worry about something or think about what might happen. Perhaps we should just turn that around a bit and be still enough to hear the messages, be attentive enough to see the signs and the synchronicities put before us. Often they are there and we just don't see them. These practices can help strengthen our spiritual intelligence.

We All Have Inner Guidance

Inner guidance is something we all possess. There is no magic way to tune in to that sense of inner wisdom and develop spiritual health. However, mindfulness studies continue to find that the practice of focusing on just one thing leads to a greater sense of self and coherence. If we are still enough, we can hear the answers. In our busy lives, we often don't take time to quiet ourselves enough to listen. Mindfulness also allows us to experience the moment without worry, self-doubt and judgment; simply observing what is, both internally and externally. The more we learn to listen to our inner guidance and follow the signs, the easier our life becomes.

"Alice" was feeling she shouldn't do a project for herself. She felt guilty for doing something just for her. Several synchronicities had occurred, telling her she should, in fact, do this project. She found something she needed for the project at the store when she was with a friend and it was on sale, so she bought it. She didn't have the right equipment to do the project, but then someone offered her what she needed. A friend even offered to help her finish the project so she didn't have to work on it alone. All of the pieces fell into place. The signs weren't obvious to her at first, but later, after she thought about it, the signs were definitely there. She didn't see them at first because her focus wasn't on them.

Inner wisdom is that part of us that is beyond our logical and conscious mind. We often feel inner wisdom as hunches, first impressions or a feeling we keep having. The first thought or impression that comes to us is usually the right one. As adults, we often second-guess, doubt and question our first thought. The first thought is our inner voice, our intuition, and our inner wisdom.

We can connect with our inner wisdom in a number of ways. Being still enough to hear our inner voice is the key. Create time and a space where we can just be and tune into our inner selves. Relaxation techniques and meditation are great ways to quiet ourselves and tune into that deeper place. As with mindfulness, letting go of all judgment is important to hearing those inner messages. Our conscious mind may be quick to say to us, "That's not right," or "It's just because I want it to be true." Trust your intuition and inner guidance.

If we are hearing or feeling messages that are neutral or coming from a place of compassion, it's our inner guidance and intuition. If the messages are negative, angry, berating or telling us we are not good enough, it is our mind, not intuition and inner knowing. The inner wisdom we all have is kind, wise and loving, not negative and berating. We feel loved and safe if we are really hearing our inner wisdom.

We experience hearing, just like visualization, in any number of ways. You may not hear voices, but you may feel something, or perhaps have a visual image, or sensation, or just an instinct. If you do feel something, trust it. Trusting our intuition is the most challenging part sometimes. Trust whatever comes to you first if it feels right. If the guidance does not make sense in our mind but still feels right, we may have to trust and go forward, not really knowing our next step. We sometimes might feel a warm feeling, a sense of peace or relief. If we truly flow with our inner wisdom, everything falls into place easily and gracefully. Our needs will be met, and often other people unexpectedly help us by paving the way.

There was a *Friends* episode in which Phoebe asked Joey questions to help him as he struggled to make a decision. She asked the questions very fast, gave him two options, and he had to choose one quickly without thinking about it. She told him to choose the first thing that came to him, since that was his inner guidance talking. It may seem silly because it was just a TV show, but the principle is there. Our gut reaction tells us something.

We feel many of our emotions and answers to our questions in our gut, or solar plexus. When we are nervous about something, that's where many of us feel the emotion. The term "gut feeling" refers to our intuition in our solar plexus, sometimes called the "abdominal brain." This brain contains neurons and neurotransmitters, just like those found in the brain in our head. The brain in our gut is also able to learn, remember and produce emotion-based feelings. That's why we have "gut feelings." The body is speaking to us, literally. Our two brains communicate back and forth via a major nerve trunk extending from the base of our brain all the way down into our abdomen. Because of this, our two brains directly influence each other. We may feel butterflies in our stomach when we are anxious, or have strange dreams or nightmares after eating foods that are hard on our stomach just before bed.

When talking to your inner wisdom, it's better to ask a small, specific question rather than going for a huge piece at once. A question like, "What do I need to do next?" or "What one little thing can I start with?" rather than a huge question like, "How can I help heal the world?" is better. You also can ask for a sign, and then pay attention.

We all have inner wisdom and intuition. It's not a special gift given only to certain people. The truth is that many times we don't listen to our intuition. Signs and messages are around us all the time, but often we are busy with day-to-day events of life and don't see them. If we are still enough, the answers will come. Meditation and quiet time are good ways to access our inner guidance. I will often pose a question during my meditation and reflection time, and if I am still enough, an answer comes, or I might get signs throughout the day. It's amazing what you notice if you are seeking an answer.

Are you are struggling with a question, like "Is this the right thing for me?" Pose the question and then ask to see signs of an answer. You can do this during your regular day or ask as you go to sleep and the answer may come in a dream state. If you want to remember your dreams, write down just a couple of words as you wake up. Once we are awake, our conscious mind kicks back in and we have trouble remembering our dreams. The subconscious mind is what is active during our dream state. The information is still there, it's just that we can't access it as easily. Have you ever had the experience when you know you dreamed about something, but couldn't remember it? Then something happens during the day that triggers the memory, you remember your dream, and the images come back to you.

Imagery Exercise: Inner Wisdom

During your waking time, you can use imagery to access your inner wisdom. This script may be helpful in walking you through the process.

"Begin by being in a comfortable position and focusing on your breathing. If you would like, circulate the healing ball of energy that goes up as you inhale, over your head, and down your spine as you exhale, taking everything that you don't need right now into the ground. Just circulate that ball of healing energy. … When you are in a comfortable place, relax enough to go somewhere in your imagination where you feel really good. It might be your favorite place, or you may have a special place that you always return to, or it may be different every time you do imagery, it doesn't matter. Go to where you feel comfortable.

"Look around, notice what's around you, what time of day it is, what you are wearing, what the temperature is like … notice everything that you can about your surroundings. Are you outside or are you indoors? Are you alone or is someone with you? Notice everything you can notice. Then just hang out there for a while. … Enjoy being in that comfortable place, and when you are ready, you can ask for your inner wisdom, your inner guidance, that image to come forth. Look around and notice if something new appears in your surroundings. It may be something that you see, it may be something that you feel or possibly hear or even smell. Just allow whatever comes to you to come to you. It's that part of us that has all the answers.

"We also all have the inner critic, so to distinguish the difference between the inner critic and the inner advisor, realize that you will feel better with the inner advisor. Your inner guidance is kind and loves you very much. Allow whatever comes to you to come. Maybe it's a person. It might be someone from your past, or an animal, or an inanimate object, a color. It doesn't really matter what comes to you. When it does, begin to notice everything about it.

"You should be able to notice that your inner advisor is kind and wise and loving, and you feel good being in that presence. Then you can begin to talk with it. If you have questions about anything, just ask. If you are not getting answers, make sure your questions are small enough. What one thing can I do first? What one thing needs to change first? Ask these questions instead of, 'How do I fix this big problem?' which may be too big of a question. Be patient and just take steps at a time. Sometimes the image that comes to us, that represents

our inner guidance, has a specific gender, sometimes not. Ask if they have a name so that you can call them by name. Ask if they're willing to meet with you again and continue your conversation. Perhaps set up a time for you to meet again. Talking with your inner advisor can be a wonderful tool that you will want to do frequently."

We all have inner guides that know us very well. Imagery, whether you're dreaming or wide awake, is a great way to access the subconscious mind. That's where all the answers are.

Many of the answers you get may not be a complete surprise to you because you probably already knew the answer at some level, or have thought it or heard of it before, but you really weren't sure. This gives you added confirmation that, at a deeper level, you really have the answer. Maybe you're pushing yourself too much or working too hard. If you talk to your inner advisor and you get those kinds of answers, it's more likely that, yes, you are pushing yourself too hard or doing too much and it's time to back off a little bit.

Without unconditional self-love, our intellect may think, "I am just not tough enough; I should be able to do this." Enjoy having conversations with your inner advisor. You may want to set up a time every day or a certain schedule to meet with your inner guide. It's a good idea to keep the appointment because it's like having a lunch date with a good friend; you don't want to stand them up. We have all the answers; we just have to ask.

Do You Believe in Angels?

Angels have been with us in every time and every culture. The word angel means messenger. Angels bring messages from the divine mind of our creator. These are gifts to us from God, sent to help us and help us remember our divine nature. They keep us out of harm's way and guide us in the areas of relationships, health, career and even finances. They may help keep us calm or heal us by allowing us to feel safe. They offer hope if we need to improve. They work in conjunction with our higher self and soul so that we are spiritually aligned.

Angels don't judge our beliefs; rather they work with our present thoughts as a way to reach us. I believe guardian angels are personally assigned to us for our entire life. Regardless of your faith, beliefs or lifestyle, everyone has at least two guardian angels according to Doreen Virtue, PhD,

The Choice is Ours

a spiritual doctor of psychology and fourth-generation metaphysician who works with the angelic, elemental and ascended master realms. Whether we choose to listen to them, however, is an entirely different matter.

One angel is your extroverted, or nudging, angel who pushes you to make choices in keeping with your highest self. She knows your talents and potential, and encourages you to shine brightly in all ways. The other guardian angel has a quiet voice. She comforts you when you are sad, lonely or disappointed. She hugs you when you don't get the job or the home that you desperately wanted, and calms you on Friday night when your date doesn't show up. You can have more than two guardian angels; in fact, Doreen believes most people have many around them. They are nondenominational and help anyone regardless of their religious or nonreligious background. Angels can help many people at the same time. We also have deceased loved ones who help us along with earth angels, who are people we may or may not know, but who just seem to show up to help us when we need them.

So how do you know if you're experiencing your angels or your imagination? Children are very good at seeing things that, as adults, we can't see. Children often see angels and have imaginary friends who are very real. As adults, we usually think it's just our imagination or something we want to hear. Angels give us signs in many ways.

Doreen Virtue has a series of oracle cards that revolve around angels. I have several sets of these cards myself. Oracle cards are an ancient, time-honored way to connect with the angels and archangels. You can't make a mistake with the oracle cards because they operate alongside the infallible Law of Attraction. This means that your question always attracts the perfect card for your answer; that is, you will pull the card that matches the vibration of the question.

If you choose to use oracle cards, simply clear the cards first because, as anything, they absorb energy. You can set an intention that the cards are clear and ready for you to use. You can ask and pray for whatever help you would like during the reading, such as confidence, clarity, compassion and so forth. Ask a question you want answered. Shuffle the cards as you would shuffle a deck of playing cards and ask for help or guidance. If one or more cards fall out of the deck while you are shuffling, place them aside because they really are part of your answer. As you shuffle, you may notice feelings, thoughts, words or visions. This divine guidance will help you further understand the cards that you draw, so pay attention to these impressions. When you stop shuffling, simply trust that you will receive divine messages. You can't make a mistake with how long you shuffle. Just do what feels right.

The Law of Attraction ensures that you always choose the correct card. You can spread the cards out and choose one, or pull the top card off the deck or take a card from the middle of the deck. There are many ways to choose a card, but don't look at it right away. Put it down for a moment, then turn it over and see the message. Consult the guidebook included with every box of cards to get a more elaborate meaning. I use my cards to set my tone for the rest of the day.

One of the most interesting things I find with oracle cards is that when I or others have used them, we seem to draw the cards we need. You may draw the same card or similar cards frequently or several times in a row for weeks at a time, and then something will happen in your life and you no longer need that answer. That card doesn't come up again.

"Kevin" kept drawing the love and romance cards. He wanted to have a relationship with a woman who was not in a position to do so. At the time, she was already in a relationship and not available to him. But he kept drawing those cards every time. One day, he found that the woman was no longer in a relationship and they were able to get together. They were very happy. He continued to draw angel cards, but the love and romance cards he had drawn before didn't come up; he drew very different cards. It's as though he didn't need those cards anymore.

When I was in the hospital after my car accident and still in a coma, my husband would draw cards using a different deck than the one I normally used. It was from the Healing with the Angels deck. He would draw the card of St. Michael the Archangel or the Guardian Angel card almost every day. When my youngest son would visit me in the hospital, he would also draw a card, and it would also be the St. Michael card. There is only one St. Michael and one Guardian Angel card in that deck, so statistically speaking, this shouldn't happen. When I was home from the hospital and doing better, my husband continued drawing cards, as did I. The St. Michael card no longer came up. It's almost as if the cards you draw are the ones you are meant to get at the time; when you don't need it anymore, you don't draw it anymore.

If you have an interest in Doreen Virtue's books or her oracle cards, you can find her at www.angeltherapy.com.

I know my life has been much richer and I have had more confidence and sense of peace since I began working more with the angels. I encourage you to find a connection to that which is outside yourself, or perhaps, deep within yourself. It's so important to connect to something, as we are never alone.

Prayer

Prayer can take many forms. One of the benefits of prayer is that it encourages us and gives us hope. Hope heals our soul where hopelessness can kill us. We probably have heard about people with life-threatening illnesses who lost hope and gave up. They did poorly, and perhaps died sooner than if they had been hopeful. Prayer can be everything from praying for ourselves or others, to focusing and giving total attention, to doing something for another, and everything in between. Meditation and prayer are often discussed together. It is said that when we pray, we often ask God for something, and during meditation, God speaks to us. Prayer can have specific words, such as those in the *Lord's Prayer;* it can be repetitive, or it can be just talking to God. Prayer also can be silent, without words, and simply a feeling.

In his book, *Prayer is Good Medicine*, Dr. Larry Dossey (www.dosseydossey.com) says that prayer is what it needs to be. Using brain-scanning technology, researchers can pinpoint which parts of the brain are active during prayer and meditation. Yoga, prayer and meditation may actually turn off the genes activated by stress.

Prayer and religion are not necessarily intertwined. How we pray is not as important as the unconditional love we integrate with the prayer, both love for others and ourselves. Prayer benefits us in many ways: reducing stress chemicals; improving healthy behaviors, such as not smoking; and enhancing spirituality, defined as a person's search for the sacred. Spirituality and the sense that there is something bigger than yourself, no matter your belief system, can be linked to less depression, increased longevity, and better medical outcomes when treatment is necessary.

Jeanna Giese's story is an example of the power of prayer. She is the only person to survive rabies without a vaccination. A bat bit Jeanna in the summer of 2004 while at church. The bat was flying around inside the church, and someone batted it down. Being an animal lover, Jeanna took the bat outside and it bit her finger. She didn't think anything of it. About three weeks later, she began having symptoms and was diagnosed with rabies. There is no known treatment for rabies, and doctors induced a deep coma in an effort to take her brain offline and allow her immune system to kick in and fight the virus.

After seven days at the very edge of death came the first signs that Jeanna's immune system was making antibodies to fight for her life. The doctors awakened her from the coma, but still didn't know if she would recover. Ten days after starting treatment, Jeanna opened her eyes. She was alive, but needed a lot of therapy to get her brain and her life back. She had to learn to speak and walk again. After a year, she was walking and talking better, and rediscovering her love of horseback riding. Today, she is an active advocate for rabies awareness. You can learn more about Jeanna at site.jeannagiese.com.

When the *New York Times* reported on the story in 2004, it said:

"Last month, doctors at the Children's Hospital of Wisconsin in Wauwatosa, a suburb of Milwaukee, put the critically ill girl into a drug-induced coma and gave her antiviral drugs, although it is not clear which, if any, of the four medicines contributed to her surprising recovery. Her father, John Giese, said he was grateful to the doctors and their novel treatment, but added that prayer had made the crucial difference. 'The day after we found out, I called on everyone we knew for prayer,' he told *The Milwaukee Journal Sentinel* this week. 'We believe a lot of that snowballed and it really made a difference.'"

I remember being a part of that prayer circle. Someone sent me an email asking me to participate. At the time I got the email, I hadn't even heard about the news. I think Jeanna's dad was right: all the prayers and good intentions sent her way helped with her miracle survival and recovery.

I had a similar experience with my own journey and brain injury. There were people praying for me that I didn't even know, and I am sure it made a difference.

Praying Rain

There are many ways to pray. Gregg Braden is an internationally known pioneer in bridging science and spirituality. He is both a scientist and an individual interested in spirituality practices around the world. He has written many books including *The Isaiah Effect*, *The God Code*, *The Divine Matrix*, and *The Spontaneous Healing of Belief: Shattering the Paradigm of False Limits* (www.greggbraden.com).

In his book *The Lost Mode of Prayer*, he talks about an experience he had in northern New Mexico. It was the early 1990s and a year of great drought. There had not been rain in many months, rivers had dried up, and the earth was parched and cracked. An American Indian friend asked Gregg if he wanted to join him in a prayer of rain. Gregg's friend asked him if he wanted to come to a place his ancestors had built, where he would pray for rain. Greg jumped at the chance to learn more about this. They drove into the desert and then walked until they came to a stone formation that looked similar to an old medicine wheel. It was a sacred ceremonial place built centuries ago. His friend said the circle of stones would provide the focus for his prayer that day, a prayer to focus on rain.

Gregg expected to see maybe a dance, some feathers, and the burning of sage as he stood back and watched. His friend took off his shoes and walked into the center of the stones. He first gave thanks to his ancestors who built this place, and then he paused for just a couple of minutes and was quiet. He walked back to Gregg and said, "Well, I'm hungry. Let's go get something to eat." Gregg was surprised. He had expected to see the stereotypical drums, dancing, chanting and praying for rain. He asked his friend what he had done when he was quiet for those few moments.

His friend said, "If I prayed for rain, it assumes that it does not exist in this moment and could not happen. The thoughts and feelings of praying for rain creates a feeling that there is not enough, a feeling of lack. So I didn't pray for rain ... I prayed rain. I took off my shoes so I could imagine the feeling of mud as it squishes between my toes when I walk through our village after it rains. I sensed the smell of our adobe houses when the rain has been showering them all day. I imagined what it feels like to walk through the cornfield that is right alongside our village, and the corn stalks were brushing my shoulders where, in actuality, the corn was not growing that year due to the drought. I felt what it feels like to already have the rain. I smelled the smells, I felt the feelings, and then I gave thanks. That was my prayer."

Feeling has an electromagnetic charge. Creating the energy of a feeling that can combine with the energy that already exists in our bodies and our universe has tremendous opportunity. It's the moment when thought, feeling and emotion become one. As Gregg's friend had felt the feeling of already having the rain, he felt grateful and knew it was here; he didn't doubt or question the possibility, he just believed and felt good.

Later that day, it rained. The village had more rain than anyone knew what to do with. Gregg noted that he has no scientific basis that this prayer about rain caused the rain that day, but it did rain – for the first time in many months.

The "lost" mode of prayer is a form of prayer that has no words, no outward expression. It is based simply in feeling. Specifically, this mode of prayer invites us to feel the appreciation and gratitude in our heart, as if our prayers are already answered, even if we don't see evidence of it.

So, why does feeling, appreciation and gratitude make such a difference?

The important part is gratitude – to be thankful wherever you are, to be grateful for being there. It's largely about energy and vibration. Everything has energy and all energy vibrates. This includes you and me, as well as all of our thoughts and feelings. Remember that every thought you have is a prayer. The positive thoughts, the things you want as though they are already here, and the negative thoughts, the worries, the fears, the fact that you don't have enough of whatever – those are really all prayers.

Journaling

I propose you also consider journaling, with a twist. An abundance-focused way to journal is to write about the future the way you want it to be. It's really writing as though you are already there; fast-forward your life by a few months, a year, two years, ten years, whatever, and pretend you are where you want to be and experience how good that feels. Imagine what it feels like to have the things that you want; there is enough money, there is enough time, there is enough love in your life, you're in the relationship you've always wanted. Whatever it is, pretend you are already there.

Remember, getting your negative or intense emotions out is important, too, so you may want to keep two journals. Keep one to write about the present or past and how you feel, expressing any negative feelings on paper. The second journal is for writing about your dreams. Journaling the future can increase your vibration, align you with your desires and manifest your dreams. Feeling good and believing you are already there is important.

It doesn't take much time, maybe five minutes a day. Just get your thoughts out and feel good. You can write about the same kinds of things or have different journals for different goals. You can write something different each day, or there may be a common theme or thought that keeps coming through. If you feel good, you are doing it right! Make it a special ritual, just for you. Consider getting yourself a journal and pen that is just for this purpose. Most of all, have fun with it. For more information on journaling in this way, visit Jeanette Maw at www.prayrainjournal.com.

I noticed something interesting when I started journaling every day. I noticed the thoughts in my journal that day came to mind several times throughout the day. I had been "praying rain" for a long time, but had never written my thoughts down before. For me, it's a fun way to start my day. You can do it anytime – it doesn't have to be in the morning – just dedicate some time every day to dream and feel good about it.

I do believe there is power in the written word. Writing down your thoughts strengthens your emotional connection. I have been through several journals because I have been doing this for a while, but every day I only spend five minutes or so. It does not take a long time, and don't worry about your penmanship, how it looks, or your grammar. Nobody has to read this anyway. In my journal, I don't even know if I can read some of the pages because my penmanship is not the best. When I start writing, I find that I feel more excited and enjoy writing about what I want for my future, as though it's already here. Once I get into the flow and the energy of this, I notice my writing gets faster and faster and my penmanship gets worse and worse. It's because I get so excited and the emotions are intense. I always end every journal page with a thank you. I am grateful for already being there!

It's just one more way to keep you in that better vibration. When you write things down, you will think about those things more throughout the day than had you just thought about them in your mind or said them aloud. Writing thoughts down gives that future picture more energy. I think more about what I write in those little moments that we all have throughout the day, those times when we are not really thinking of anything and something pops into our head. That's what it was like with this. The things I had written about that day or just recently started popping into my head more and more.

Of course, as you are writing these things down, it's meant to make you feel good because you are pretending you already have what you want. You are daydreaming and fantasizing about already being there and being thankful for that.

My husband and I did this after the 2010 earthquake in Chile. There was fear the quake may cause a tsunami to head toward the Hawaiian Islands, and we were due to go on vacation to there in a few weeks. We were concerned that the places we are used to seeing when we are on the island of Kauai might not be the same if a tsunami hit the islands. I suggested to my husband that we pray rain. So we imagined ourselves lying on the beach, saying to each other how thankful we are that everything is just like we left it the last time we were here. We imagined that everything is the same, and we felt the feeling of lying on the beach, experiencing the warm sun and sand, and smelling the aromas of Kauai. We felt appreciation and were so thankful.

Of course, I wrote about it in my journal as well. Feeling gratitude, writing about things, talking about things as though you are already there, has a huge impact on your energy. Anything that has huge impact like that on your energy is going to affect your vibration in a very positive way.

As it turned out, the wave was only three feet high when it arrived at the Hawaiian Islands, and there was no damage.

Benefit of a Daily Routine

There is a benefit to beginning a daily routine. It should fit your life and be something you look forward to. If you dread doing something or don't feel you can take the time, it will not be beneficial for you.

"Emily" has a lot of stress at work, and noted that in the past this would have bothered her to the point of emotional eating and gaining weight. She would then feel like a failure and would be upset with herself. She noted that things have changed and she feels much more confident, peaceful and sure that everything will work out fine. The work stress is still there and many of her colleagues are really struggling, but she feels in a better place emotionally. When I asked her what she thought made the difference in how work affects her, she told me about her morning routine. For her whole life she had been struggling with self-confidence, and work had always been her biggest challenge.

Emily starts every morning with a routine. She gets up early every morning and her husband brings her decaf coffee. She sits in her favorite chair, spending time meditating and just being. She notices the birds outside the window and feels thankful for her life. While she is meditating, she acknowledges the thoughts that come to her and them lets them go, coming from a non-scolding, loving place. She often focuses on her breath or the birds; sometimes she just listens to the silence in the house before the kids are up. Then she draws a few angel cards. The angel cards are a way to give her a thought to start her day. She may read some Bible passages as well, and reflect on them. She says she sees more signs and messages from God and the angels when she starts her day this way.

She spends some time reflecting and feeling appreciation for all she has. Then she writes about the future in her journal, and feels as though she is already there. She feels joy, excitement and abundance as she is writing. She has a special pen she uses, and this is her time write about her dreams. The future that Emily writes about is filled with happiness and everything she wants, and she feels like she's really experiencing this as though it's happening now. She feels so excited as she is writing that it's as if the pen can't slide across the paper fast enough. She gets to the bottom of the page and squeezes in a "Thank You" of gratitude. She feels the positive energy, good vibration and happiness as she imagines she is already there.

Her whole morning routine takes only about forty-five minutes. She feels good doing this for herself, since she feels this makes her a better person to be around. Her kids and colleagues have noticed the new person she has become. Emily finds she is not the same if she doesn't start out every day like this. Her husband and people who know her well have commented that they see a difference.

Emily ends her day by thinking of all the things she is thankful for that day. She feels she has never before felt this sense of joy and confidence in her life. She begins and ends each day on a good note, and she is convinced it has made a huge difference for her.

I think that we are different when we start our day this way versus when we don't. It's just something to think about and another thing that may help you get to that positive place you want to be.

What can you do? What can you fit into your day? You don't have to do all this in the morning, but I would recommend you think about a daily practice, something you can fit into your day somehow. It doesn't matter what time of day it is, but what can you add that helps you feel good? Think about the things that you want, and daydream while imagining you are already there.

What can you do? Would journaling be the right thing for you? Would spending a little time meditating be the right thing for you? Or would just having different thoughts be helpful? It's always good to start with just being aware of what is. Be aware of your thoughts, your feelings, what you are thinking throughout the day, the people around you, and what you see. We all receive messages and signs every day; it's those little synchronicities in life. Very often we just don't see them. But, if you are consciously looking for something, you will notice because your attention is focused on it. So think about a daily practice you could begin.

Summary and Suggestions

Unconditional love means that you recognize the divine within yourself as well as all people. Sometimes loving ourselves unconditionally is the most challenging task. Spirituality is the way we find meaning, hope, comfort and inner peace in our lives. It is how we know we are loved, safe and protected.

- Practice being still enough to hear your inner voice.
- Use imagery, meditation, prayer or quiet reflection time to access our inner wisdom.
- Communicate with God, the angels, whatever that greater power is for you.
- Draw angel cards or read passages from a Bible or other text to start your day on a positive note. Begin a daily practice. Choose the things you can do and want to do on a daily basis. You don't have to do everything at once; you can build on this and add things along the way.

Conclusion

Plan Your Daily Practice

My hope is that you incorporate some of the tools I've given throughout this book into your daily practice. You can find more information on the websites and in the suggested reading I've listed at the end of this book as well. Reserve some quiet time and take an inventory of the things you think about that don't make you feel good. Maybe it's something from your childhood, family, school years or a previous job; maybe it's something said to you a long time ago, and perhaps you can still hear that person saying it now and then. Practice with tools I've described such as affirmations, journaling, EFT, the two-minute relaxation, and taking in the love technique are all good ways to reorganize those limiting beliefs and change your vibration.

Be aware of your thoughts. What issues are you exposed to every day where you could ask the so-what question? Notice if it's hard for you to let go of things, and ask why. Notice situations where you could choose to feel a different way. Pay attention to how you are choosing to take care of your body. If you are not choosing healthy things, ask why. Do you value yourself? Do you accept yourself as you are? Do you feel worthy? Would you treat someone else better or differently than you treat yourself?

What choices are you making about how much water you drink, what you eat, and how you move your body? Basically, do you love yourself unconditionally? Maybe you could begin to take better care of yourself.

Be aware of how much time you feel good and how much of the time you don't. Maybe give it a percentage. See yourself on that twelve-inch ruler.

Are you on the zero- to six-inch end or are you on the six- to twelve-inch side? Are you more toward something you don't want or more toward something you do want? Notice how much of the time you head in the right direction. If there are things keeping you stuck, work on some of those limiting beliefs using techniques in this book or get some professional help if necessary. You may want to start some sort of gratitude practice. Be grateful for things, especially right before you go to sleep. It's a great time to do this. You may want to begin a future journaling practice, journaling as though you are already there, where you want to be; how good it feels and how thankful you are. Of course, you want to surround yourself most of the time with good energy. Surround yourself with people who make you feel good, doing things that make you feel good. Perhaps start a daily practice of your own: meditating, journaling, drawing angel cards, or reading passages from the Bible or some other text. You need something to start your day on a good note. You will feel yourself changing if you do something like this every day. Soon things won't bother you as much, and you will be a happier, healthier, more abundant person. End your day with good thoughts and feelings. Perhaps taking inventory of your life or the day, and feeling the sense of gratitude. There is something greater than us, a greater plan. Take comfort in believing this. Feel empowered knowing that you have choice and inner wisdom that you can call on as well. I hope I have given you some tools and some things to think about. Take what works for you and let go of the rest. Above all, love yourself and believe that you can have the life you want!

About the Author

Bonnie Groessl, MSN, is board certified by the American Nurses Credentialing Center as a Family Nurse Practitioner and has additional training in integrative medicine, mind-body techniques, energy work, as well as headache and chronic-pain management. She owns The Bridge to Health, an integrative healing center in Green Bay, Wisconsin. Bonnie is recognized as an expert in helping people make changes to achieve their goals. Her focus is on providing an integrative, holistic approach to people with chronic emotional and physical pain. Patients learn tools that bring together mind-body medicine, nutrition, energy medicine and spirituality to help them enjoy the lives they deserve.

Bonnie is active in public speaking and presenting workshops for professionals and the public. She lives in Green Bay with her husband, Mike, and has two grown sons, happily living their own lives.

To stay in touch with Bonnie, you can sign up for her emailing list on any of her websites:

www.BonnieGroessl.com
www.TheBridgetoHealth.org
www.MyRelaxationCenter.com
www.WordsforWellness.com

Resources

Suggested Reading

Amen, Daniel, and Lisa Routh. *Healing Anxiety and Depression.* New York: G.P. Putnam's Sons/Penguin Group, 2003.

Crowley, Chris, and Lodge, Henry. *Younger Next Year: Live Strong, Fit, and Sexy-Until You're 80 and Beyond.* New York: Workman Publishing, 2004.

Dyer, Wayne. *10 Secrets for Success and Inner Peace.* California: Hay House Inc. 2001.

Eden, Donna, and David Feinstein. *Energy Medicine: Balancing Your Body's Energies for Optimal Health, Joy and Vitality.* New York: Penguin Putnam Inc., 1998.

MacWilliam, Lyle. *Comparative Guide to Nutritional Supplements, 4th ed.* Canada: NutriSearch Corp. and Northern Dimensions Publishing, 2007.

Ruiz, Don Miguel. *The Four Agreements.* California:Amber-Allen Publishing, Inc. 1997

Schubiner, Howard, with Michael Betzold. *Unlearn Your Pain: A 28-Day Process to Reprogram Your Bain..* Missouri: Mind Body Publishing, 2010

Shealy, C. Norman. *Life Beyond 100: Secrets of the Fountain of Youth.* New York: Penguin Group Inc., 2005.

Shimoff, Marci, with Carol Kline. *Love for No Reason: 7 Steps to Creating a Life of Unconditional Love.* New York: Free Press/Simon & Schuster Inc., 2010.

Siegel, Bernie. *Love, Medicine and Miracles: Lessons Learned about Self-Healing from a Surgeon's Experience with Exceptional Patients.* New York: Harper & Row Publishers Inc., 1986.

Useful Websites

For more information, visit the author's membership site at www.BonnieGroessl.com

Animoto (slide-show creator) www.animoto.com

Braden, Gregg, www.greggbraden.com

Chopra, Deepak, www.deepakchopra.com

Church, Dawson, www.dawsonchurch.com

Lipton, Bruce, www.brucelipton.com

Eden, Donna, www.innersource.net

Emotional Freedom Techniques (EFT information and products) www.thetappingsolution.com

Emotional Freedom Techniques (EFT information, products, and research) www.eftuniverse.com

Hay, Louise, www.louisehay.com

Hicks, Esther, and Jerry Hicks, Abraham-Hicks Publications, www.abraham-hicks.com

Institute of HeartMath, www.heartmath.org

Look, Carol, EFT, www.carollookeft.com

Maw, Jeanette, www.prayrainjournal.com

Mind Movies (visualization tool with images, music and affirmations) www.mindmovies.com

Naparstek, Belelruth, audios, www.healthjourneys.com

Proctor, Bob, www.bobproctor.com

PSYCH-K®, www.dev.psych-k.com

Rossman, Dr. Martin, *Guided Imagery for Self-Healing,* www.thehealingmind.org

Ruiz, don Miguel, www.miguelruiz.com

Schubiner, Dr. Howard, www.unlearnyourpain.com

Shealy, Dr. Norm, www.normshealy.com

Shimoff, Marci, www.thelovebook.com

Source for Objective Science-based DHA/EPA Omega-3 Information, www.dhaomega3.org

Source for Vitamin D, www.vitaminDcouncil.org

Virtue, Doreen, www.angeltherapy.com

Weil, Dr. Andrew, www.drweil.com

Links to all the websites found in this book are located on Bonnie's website www.bonniegroessl.com

References

Amen, Daniel. *Change Your Brain, Change Your Life: The Breakthrough Program for Conquering Anxiety, Depression, Obsessiveness, Anger, and Impulsiveness.* New York: Three Rivers Press, 1998.

Amen, Daniel, and Lisa Routh. *Healing Anxiety and Depression.* New York: G.P. Putnam's Sons/Penguin Group, 2003.

Braden, Gregg, *Secrets of the Lost Mode of Prayer: The Hidden Power of Beauty, Blessings, Wisdom, and Hurt* (2006, Hay House Inc. Carlsbad, CA)

Childre, Doc, and Howard Martin, with Donna Beech, *The Heart Math Solution: The Institute of HeartMath's revolutionary Program for Engaging the Power of the Heart's Intelligence.* New York: HarperCollins, 1999.

Church, Dawson. *The Genie in Your Genes: Epigenetic Medicine and the New Biology of Intention.* California: Elite Books, 2007.

Dale, Cyndi. *The Subtle Body: An Encyclopedia of Your Energetic Anatomy.* Colorado: Sounds True Inc., 2009.

Dean, Carolyn. *The Magnesium Miracle.* New York: Ballantine Books/Random House Inc., 2007.

Doidge, Norman. *The Brain That Changes Itself: Stories of Personal Triumph from the Frontiers of Brain Science.* New York: Viking Penguin/Penguin Group, 2007.

Dossey, Larry. *Prayer is Good Medicine: How to Reap the Healing Benefits of Prayer.* New York: HarperCollins Publishers Inc., 1996.

Hannaford, Carla. *Smart Moves: Why Learning is Not All in Your Head.* Virginia: Great Ocean Publishers Inc., 1995.

Hanson, Rick, with Richard Mendius. *Buddha's Brain: The Practical Neuroscience of Happiness, Love, and Wisdom*. California: New Harbinger Publications Inc., 2009.

Hay, Louise, *You Can Heal Your Life* (2004, Hay House Inc. Carlsbad, CA)

Hicks, Esther, and Jerry Hicks, *Ask and It Is Given: Learning to Manifest Your Desires* (2004, Hay House Inc. Carlsbad, CA)

Kabat-Zinn, Jon. *Full Catastrophe Living: Using the Wisdom of Your Body and Mind to Face Stress, Pain, and Illness*. New York: Dell Publishing/Random House Inc., 1990.

Kabat-Zinn, Jon. *Wherever You Go, There You Are: Mindfulness Meditation in Everyday Life*. New York: Hyperion, 1994.

Lipton, Bruce. *The Biology of Belief: Unleashing the Power of Consciousness, Matter, and Miracles*. California: Mountain of Love Productions/Hay House Inc., 2005.

O'Hanlon, William Hudson, and Michael Martin. *Solution-Oriented Hypnosis: An Ericksonian Approach*. New York: W.W. Norton & Co., 1992.

Promislow, Sharon. *Making the Brain/Body Connection: A Playful Guide to Releasing Mental, Physical, and Emotional Blocks to Success*. British Columbia: Enhanced Learning & Integration Inc., 2005.

Ratey, John, with Eric Hagerman. *Spark: The Revolutionary New Science of Exercise and the Brain*. New York: Little, Brown and Co., 2008.

Rossman, Martin L. *Guided Imagery for Self-Healing*. Copyright © 2000. Reprinted with permission of H J Kramer/New World Library, Novato, CA. www.newworldlibrary.com.

Strand, Ray D., with Donna Wallace. *Healthy for Life: Developing Healthy Lifestyles That Have a Side Effect of Permanent Fat Loss*. South Dakota: Health Concepts Publishing/Real Life Press, 2003.

Virtue, Doreen, *How to Hear Your Angels* (2007, Hay House Inc. Carlsbad, CA)

Virtue, Doreen, *The Angel Therapy Handbook* (2011, Hay House Inc. Carlsbad, CA)

Weil, Andrew. *8 Weeks to Optimum Health: A Proven Program for Taking Full Advantage of Your Body's Natural Healing Power*. New York: Ballantine Books/Random House Inc., 1997.

Weil, Andrew. *Spontaneous Healing: How to Discover and Embrace Your Body's Natural Ability to Maintain and Heal Itself.* New York: Ballantine Book/Random House Inc., 1995.

Willett, Walter, with Patrick Skerrett. *Eat, Drink, and Be Healthy: The Harvard Medical School Guide to Health Eating.* New York: Free Press/Simon & Schuster Inc., 2001.

Williams, Robert. *Psych-K: The Missing Peace in Your Life!* Colorado: Myrddin Publications, 2004.

CPSIA information can be obtained at www.ICGtesting.com
Printed in the USA
LVOW080759130112

263431LV00001B/37/P